Charles Lamb, Percy Hetherington Fitzgerald

The Art of the Stage as Set Out in Lamb's Dramatic Essays

Charles Lamb, Percy Hetherington Fitzgerald

The Art of the Stage as Set Out in Lamb's Dramatic Essays

ISBN/EAN: 9783337303976

Printed in Europe, USA, Canada, Australia, Japan

Cover: Foto ©Thomas Meinert / pixelio.de

More available books at **www.hansebooks.com**

LAMB'S DRAMATIC ESSAYS

WITH A COMMENTARY

BY

PERCY FITZGERALD, M.A., F.S.A.

London

REMINGTON & CO., PUBLISHERS

HENRIETTA STREET, COVENT GARDEN

1885

INSCRIBED

WITH MUCH REGARD

TO

EDWARD F. S. PIGOTT

EXAMINER OF PLAYS)

ABSTRACT OF CONTENTS

CRITICISMS OF DRAMATIC WRITERS

THE COMMENTARY

THE ART OF THE STAGE

AS SET FORTH IN THE DRAMATIC ESSAYS
OF CHARLES LAMB

—◆►—o—◄◆—

THE TRAGEDIES OF SHAKSPEARE,
CONSIDERED WITH REFERENCE TO THEIR
FITNESS FOR STAGE REPRESENTATION

TAKING a turn the other day in the Abbey, I
was struck with the affected attitude of a figure,
which I do not remember to have seen before, and
which upon examination proved to be a whole-length
of the celebrated Mr Garrick. Though I would not
go so far with some good Catholics abroad as to
shut players altogether out of consecrated ground,
yet I own I was not a little scandalised at the introduction of theatrical airs and gestures into a
place set apart to remind us of the saddest realities.

A

Going nearer, I found inscribed under this harlequin
figure the following lines :—

> 'To paint fair Nature, by divine command,
> Her magic pencil in his glowing hand,
> A Shakspeare rose ; then, to expand his fame
> Wide o'er this breathing world, a Garrick came,
> Though sunk in death the forms the Poet drew,
> The Actor's genius bade them breathe anew ;
> Though, like the bard himself, in night they lay,
> Immortal Garrick call'd them back to day ;
> And till Eternity with power sublime
> Shall mark the mortal hour of hoary Time,
> Shakspeare and Garrick like twin stars shall shine,
> And earth irradiate with a beam divine.'

It would be an insult to my readers' understand-
ings to attempt anything like a criticism on this
farrago of false thoughts and nonsense. But the
reflection it led me into was a kind of wonder, how,
from the days of the actor here celebrated to our
own, it should have been the fashion to compliment
every performer in his turn, that has had the luck
to please the Town in any of the great characters of
Shakspeare, with the notion of possessing a *mind
congenial with the poet's :* how people should come
thus unaccountably to confound the power of
originating poetical images and conceptions with
the faculty of being able to read or recite the same
when put into words ;* or what connection that

---

* It is observable that we fall into this confusion only in *dramatic*
recitations. We never dream that the gentleman who reads Lucretius
in public with great applause is therefore a great poet and philosopher ;
nor do we find that Tom Davies, the bookseller, who is recorded to have
recited the Paradise Lost better than any man in England in his day
(though I cannot help thinking there must be some mistake in this
tradition) was therefore, by his intimate friends, set upon a level with
Milton.

absolute mastery over the heart and soul of man, which a great dramatic poet possesses, has with those low tricks upon the eye and ear, which a player by observing a few general effects, which some common passion, as grief, anger, &c., usually has upon the gestures and exterior, can so easily compass. To know the internal workings and movements of a great mind, of an Othello or a Hamlet for instance, the *when* and the *why* and the *how far* they should be moved; to what pitch a passion is becoming; to give the reins and to pull in the curb exactly at the moment when the drawing in or the slackening is most graceful; seems to demand a reach of intellect of a vastly different extent from that which is employed upon the bare imitation of the signs of these passions in the countenance or gesture, which signs are usually observed to be most lively and emphatic in the weaker sort of minds, and which signs can, after all, but indicate some passion, as I said before,—anger, or grief, generally; but of the motives and grounds of the passion, wherein it differs from the same passion in low and vulgar natures, of these the actor can give no more idea by his face or gesture than the eye (without a metaphor) can speak, or the muscles utter intelligible sounds. But such is the instantaneous nature of the impressions which we take in at the eye and ear at a play-house, compared with the slow apprehension oftentimes of the understanding in reading, that we are apt not only

to sink the play-writer in the consideration which
we pay to the actor, but even to identify in our
minds, in a perverse manner, the actor with the
character which he represents.   It is difficult for a
frequent play-goer to disembarrass the idea of
Hamlet from the person and voice of Mr K⸺
We speak of Lady Macbeth, while we are in reality
thinking of Mrs S⸺ Nor is this confusion
incidental alone to unlettered persons, who, not
possessing the advantage of reading, are necessarily
dependent upon the stage-player for all the pleasure
which they can receive from the drama, and to
whom the very idea of *what an author is* cannot
be made comprehensible without some pain and
perplexity of mind : the error is one from which
persons otherwise not meanly lettered, find it almost
impossible to extricate themselves.

Never let me be so ungrateful as to forget the
very high degree of satisfaction which I received
some years back from seeing for the first time a
tragedy of Shakspeare's performed, in which those
two great performers sustained the principal parts.
It seemed to embody and realise conceptions which
had hitherto assumed no distinct shape.   But dearly
do we pay all our life after for this juvenile pleasure,
this sense of distinctness.   When the novelty is
past, we find to our cost that instead of realising
an idea, we have only materialised and brought
down a fine vision to the standard of flesh and
blood.   We have let go a dream, in quest of an
unattainable substance.

How cruelly this operates upon the mind, to
have its free conceptions thus cramped and pressed
down to the measure of a strait-lacing actuality,
may be judged from that delightful sensation of
freshness, with which we turn to those plays of
Shakspeare which have escaped being performed,
and to those passages in the acting plays of the
same writer which have happily been left out in
the performance. How far the very custom of
hearing any thing *spouted*, withers and blows upon
a fine passage, may be seen in those speeches from
Henry the Fifth, &c., which are current in the
mouths of schoolboys, from their being to be found
in *Enfield's Speaker*, and such kind of books. I
confess myself utterly unable to appreciate that
celebrated soliloquy in Hamlet, beginning ' To be,
or not to be,' or to tell whether it be good, bad, or
indifferent, it has been so handled and pawed about
by declamatory boys and men, and torn so in-
humanly from its living place and principle of con-
tinuity in the play, till it is become to me a perfect
dead member.

It may seem a paradox, but I cannot help being
of opinion that the plays of Shakspeare are less
calculated for performance on a stage than those of
almost any other dramatist whatever. Their distinguishing excellence is a reason that they should
be so; there is so much in them, which comes not
under the province of acting, with which eye, and
tone, and gesture, have nothing to do.

The glory of the scenic art is to personate passion,

and the turns of passion; and the more coarse and
palpable the passion is, the more hold upon the eyes
and ears of the spectators and performer obviously
possesses. For this reason, scolding scenes, scenes
where two persons talk themselves into a fit of fury,
and then in a surprising manner talked themselves
out of it again, have always been the most popular
upon our stage. And the reason is plain, because
the spectators are here most palpably appealed to,
they are the proper judges in this war of words,
they are the legitimate ring that should be formed
round such 'intellectual prize-fighters.' Talking is
the direct object of the imitation here. But in all
the best dramas, and in Shakspeare's above all, how
obvious it is, that the form of *speaking*, whether it
be in soliloquy or dialogue is only a medium, and
often a highly artificial one for putting the reader or
spectator into possession of that knowledge of the
inner structure and workings of mind in a character
which he could otherwise never have arrived at in
that form of composition by any gift short of
intuition. We do here as we do with novels
written in the *epistolary form*. How many impro-
prieties, perfect solecisms in letter writing, do we
put up with in *Clarissa*, and other books, for the
sake of the delight which that form upon the whole
gives us!

But the practice of stage representation reduces
every thing to a controversy of elocution. Every
character, from the boisterous blasphemings of
Bajazet to the shrinking timidity of womanhood,

must play the orator. The love dialogues of Romeo
and Juliet, those silver-sweet sounds of lovers'
tongues by night; the more intimate and sacred
sweetness of nuptial colloquy between an Othello
or a Posthumus with their married wives; all those
delicacies which are so delightful in the reading, as
when we read of those youthful dalliances in
Paradise—

> 'As beseem'd
> Fair couple link'd in happy nuptial league,
> Alone;'

by the inherent fault of stage representation, how
are these things sullied and turned from their very
nature by being exposed to a large assembly; when
such speeches as Imogen addresses to her lord come
drawling out of the mouth of a hired actress, whose
courtship, though nominally addressed to the personated Posthumus, is manifestly aimed at the
spectators, who are to judge of her endearments
and her returns of love!

The character of Hamlet is perhaps that by
which, since the days of Betterton, a succession of
popular performers have had the greatest ambition
to distinguish themselves. The length of the part
may be one of their reasons. But for the character
itself, we find it in a play, and therefore we judge
it a fit subject of dramatic representation. The
play itself abounds in maxims and reflections
beyond any other, and therefore we consider it as a
proper vehicle for conveying moral instruction.
But Hamlet himself—what does he suffer mean-

while by being dragged forth as a public school-
master, to give lectures to the crowd! Why, nine
parts in ten of what Hamlet does, are transactions
between himself and his moral sense; they are the
effusions of his solitary musings, which he retires
to holes and corners and the most sequestered parts
of the palace to pour forth; or rather, they are the
silent meditations with which his bosom is bursting,
reduced to *words* for the sake of the reader, who
must else remain ignorant of what is passing there.

These profound sorrows, these light-and-noise-
abhorring ruminations, which the tongue scarce
dares utter to deaf walls and chambers, how can
they be represented by a gesticulating actor, who
comes and mouths them out before an audience
making four hundred people his confidants at once!
I say not that it is the fault of the actor so to do;
he must pronounce them *ore rotundo*; he must
accompany them with his eye; he must insinuate
them into his auditory by some trick of eye, tone,
or gesture,—or he fails. *He must be thinking all
the while of his appearance, because he knows that
all the while the spectators are judging of it.* And
this is the way to represent the shy, negligent, retiring Hamlet!

It is true that there is no other mode of conveying a vast quantity of thought and feeling to a
great portion of the audience, who otherwise would
never earn it for themselves by reading; and the
intellectual acquisition gained this way may, for
aught I know, be inestimable; but I am not arguing

that Hamlet should not be acted, but how much Hamlet is made another thing by being acted. I have heard much of the wonders which Garrick performed in this part; but as I never saw him, I must have leave to doubt whether the representation of such a character came within the province of his art. Those who tell me of him, speak of his eye, of the magic of his eye, and of his commanding voice; —physical properties, vastly desirable in an actor, and without which he can never insinuate meaning into an auditory: but what have they to do with Hamlet; what have they to do with intellect? In fact, the things aimed at in theatrical representation are to arrest the spectator's eye upon the form and the gesture, and so to gain a more favourable hearing to what is spoken: it is not what the character is, but how he looks; not what he says, but how he speaks it. I see no reason to think that if the play of Hamlet were written over again by some such writer as Banks or Lillo, retaining the process of the story, but totally omitting all the poetry of it, all the divine features of Shakspeare, his stupendous intellect, and only taking care to give us enough of passionate dialogue, which neither Banks nor Lillo was ever at a loss to furnish; I see not how the effect could be much different upon an audience, nor how the actor has it in his power to represent Shakspeare to us differently from his representation of Banks or Lillo. Hamlet would still be a youthful accomplished prince, and must be gracefully personated; he

might be puzzled in his mind, wavering in his conduct, seemingly cruel to Ophelia; he might see a
ghost, and start at it, and address it kindly when
he found it to be his father; all this in the poorest
and most homely language of the servilest creeper
after nature that ever consulted the palate of an
audience, without troubling Shakspeare for the
matter; and I see not but there would be room for
all the power which an actor has, to display itself.
All the passions and changes of passion might remain; for those are much less difficult to write or
act than is thought; it is a trick easy to be attained, it is but rising or falling a note or two in
the voice, a whisper with a significant foreboding
look to announce its approach, and so contagious
the counterfeit appearance of any emotion is, that
let the words be what they will, the look and tone
shall carry it off and make it pass for deep skill in
the passions.

It is common for people to talk of Shakspeare's
plays being *so* *natural*, that every body can
understand him.   They are natural indeed, they
are grounded deep in nature, so deep that
the depth of them lies out of the reach of most of
us.   You shall hear the same persons say that George
Barnwell is very natural, and Othello is very
natural, that they are both very deep; and to them
they are the same kind of thing.   At the one they
sit and shed tears, because a good sort of young man
is tempted by a naughty woman to commit a *trifling*

peccadillo, the murder of an uncle or so,* that is all, and so comes to an untimely end, which is *so moving ;* and at the other, because a blackamoor in a fit of jealousy kills his innocent white wife ; and the odds are that ninety-nine out of a hundred would willing behold the same catastrophe happen to both the heroes, and have thought the rope more due to Othello than to Barnwell. For of the texture of Othello's mind, the inward construction marvellously laid open with all its strengths and weaknesses, its heroic confidences and its human misgivings, its agonies of hate springing from the depths of love, they see no more than the spectators at a cheaper rate, who pay their pennies a-piece to look through the man's telescope in Leicester Fields, see into the inward plot and topography of the moon. Some dim thing or other they see ; they see an actor personating a passion, of grief, or anger, for instance, and they recognise it as a copy of the usual external effects of such passions ; or at least as being true to *that symbol of the emotion*

---

* If this note could hope to meet the eye of any of the Managers, I would intreat and beg of them, in the name of both the Galleries, that this insult upon the morality of the common people of London should cease to be eternally repeated in the holiday weeks. Why are the 'Prentices of this famous and well-governed city, instead of an amusement, to be treated over and over again with a nauseous sermon of George Barnwell? Why *at the end of their vistoes* are we to place the *gallows*? Were I an uncle, I should not much like a nephew of mine to have such an example placed before his eyes. It is really making uncle-murder too trivial to exhibit it as done upon such slight motives ;—it is attributing too much to such characters as Millwood :—it is putting things into the heads of good young men, which they would never otherwise have dreamed of. Uncles that think anything of their lives should fairly petition the Chamberlain against it.

which passes current at the theatre for it, for it is
often no more than that; but of the grounds of the
passion, its correspondence to a great or heroic
nature, which is the only worthy object of tragedy,
—that common auditors know any thing of this, or
can have any such notions dinned into them by the
mere strength of an actor's lungs,—that apprehensions foreign to them should be thus infused
into them by storm, I can neither believe, nor
understand how it can be possible.

We talk of Shakspeare's admirable observation of
life, when we should feel, that not from a pretty
inquisition into those cheap and every-day
characters which surrounded him, as they surround
us, but from his own mind, which was, to borrow a
phrase of Ben Jonson's, the very 'sphere of
humanit,' he fetched those images of virtue and of
knowledge, of which every one of us recognising a
part, think we comprehend in our natures the
whole; and oftentimes mistake the powers which
he positively creates in us, for nothing more than
indigenous faculties of our own minds, which only
waited the application of corresponding virtues in
him to return a full and clear echo of the same.

To return to Hamlet—Among the distinguishing
features of that wonderful character, one of the
most interesting (yet painful) is that soreness of
mind which makes him treat the intrusions
of Polonius with harshness, and that asperity
which he puts on in his interviews with Ophelia.
These tokens of an unhinged mind (if they be not

mixed in the latter case with a profound artifice
of love, to alienate Ophelia by affected discourtesies,
so to prepare her mind for the breaking off of that
loving intercourse, which can no longer find a place
amidst business so serious as that which he has to
do) are parts of his character, which to reconcile
with our admiration of Hamlet, the most patient
consideration of his situation is no more than
necessary; they are what we *forgive afterwards*,
and explain by the whole of his character, but *at
the time* they are harsh and unpleasant. Yet such
is the actor's necessity of giving strong blows to
the audience, that I have never seen a player in
this character who did not exaggerate and strain
to the utmost these ambiguous features — these
temporary deformities in the character. They
make him express a vulgar scorn at Polonius
which utterly degrades his gentility, and which
no explanation can render palatable; they make
him show contempt, and curl up the nose at
Ophelia's father—contempt in its very grossest
and most hateful form; but they get applause by
it: it is natural, people say; that is, the words are
scornful, and the actor expresses scorn, and that
they can judge of: but why so much scorn, and of
that sort, they never think of asking.

So to Ophelia.—All the Hamlets that I have
ever seen, rant and rave at her as if she had
committed some great crime, and the audience
are highly pleased, because the words of the part
are satirical, and they are enforced by the strongest

expression of satirical indignation of which the
face and voice are capable. But then, whether
Hamlet is likely to have put on such brutal
appearances to a lady whom he loved so dearly,
is never thought on. The truth is, that in all
such deep affections as had subsisted between
Hamlet and Ophelia, there is a stock of *supererogatory love*, (if I may venture to use the expression,) which in any great grief of heart, especially
where that which preys upon the mind cannot be
communicated, confers a kind of indulgence upon
the grieved party to express itself, even to its
heart's dearest object, in the language of a temporary alienation; but it is not alienation, it is
purely a distraction, and so it always makes itself
to be felt by that object; it is not anger, but grief
assuming the appearance of anger—love awkwardly
counterfeiting hate, as sweet countenances when
they try to frown; but such sternness and fierce
disgust as Hamlet is made to show, is no counterfeit, but the real face of absolute aversion—of
irreconcileable alienation. It may be said he puts
on the madman; but then he should only so far
put on this counterfeit lunacy as his own real
distraction will give him leave; that is, incompletely, imperfectly; not in that confirmed, practised way, like a master of his art, or as Dame
Quickly would say, 'like one of those harlotry
players.'

I mean no disrespect to any actor, but the sort
of pleasure which Shakspeare's plays give in the

acting seems to me not at all to differ from that which the audience receive from those of other writers; and, *they being in themselves essentially so different from all others*, I must conclude that there is something in the nature of acting which levels all distinctions. And, in fact, who does not speak indifferently of the Gamester and of Macbeth as fine stage performances, and praise the Mrs Beverley in the same way as the Lady Macbeth of Mrs S——? Belvidera, and Calista, and Isabella, and Euphrasia, are they less liked than Imogen, or than Juliet, or than Desdemona? Are they not spoken of and remembered in the same way? Is not the female performer as great (as they call it) in one as in the other? Did not Garrick shine, and was he not ambitious of shining, in every drawling tragedy that his wretched day produced,—the productions of the Hills, and the Murphys, and the Browns? and shall we have that honour to dwell in our minds for ever as an inseparable concomitant with Shakspeare? A kindred mind! Oh, who can read that affecting sonnet of Shakspeare's which alludes to his profession as a player :—

> 'Oh for my sake do you with Fortune chide,
> The guilty goddess of my harmless deeds,
> That did not better for my life provide
> Than public means which public custom breeds;
> Thence comes it that my name receives a brand;
> And almost thence my nature is subdued
> To what it works in, like the dyer's hand.'—

*, Or that other confession :—

> ' Alas ! 'tis true, I have gone here and there,
> And make myself a motley to thy view,
> Gored mine own thoughts, sold cheap what is most dear '—

Who can read these instances of jealous self-watch-
fulness in our sweet Shakspeare, and dream of any
congeniality between him and one that, by every
tradition of him, appear to have been as mere a
player as ever existed; to have had his mind
tainted with the lowest players' vices, envy and
jealousy, and miserable cravings after applause;
one who in the exercise of his profession was
jealous even of the women-performers that stood
in his way; a manager full of managerial tricks
and stratagems and finesse; that any resemblance
should be dreamed of between him and Shakspeare,
—Shakspeare who, in the plenitude and consciousness of his own powers, could with that noble
modesty, which we can neither imitate nor appreciate, express himself thus of his own sense of
his own defects :—

> ' Wishing me like to one more rich in hope,
> Featured like him, like him with friends possest ;
> Desiring *this man's art, and that man's scope.*'

I am almost disposed to deny to Garrick the
merit of being an admirer of Shakspeare. A true
lover of his excellences he certainly was not ; for
would any true lover of them have admitted into

his matchless scenes such ribald trash as Tate and Cibber, and the rest of them, that

'With their darkness durst affront his light,'

have foisted into the acting plays of Shakspeare? I believe it impossible that he could have had a proper reverence for Shakspeare, and have condescended to go through that interpolated scene in Richard the Third, in which Richard tries to break his wife's heart by telling her he loves another woman, and says, 'if she survives this she is immortal.' Yet I doubt not he delivered this vulgar stuff with as much anxiety of emphasis as any of the genuine part: and for acting, it is as well calculated as any. But we have seen the part of Richard lately produce great fame to an actor by his manner of playing it, and it lets us into the secret of acting, and of popular judgments of Shakspeare derived from acting. Not one of the spectators who have witnessed Mr C.'s exertions in that part, but has come away with a proper conviction that Richard is a very wicked man, and kills little children in their beds, with something like the pleasure which the giants and ogres in children's books are represented to have taken in that practice; moreover, that he is very close and shrewd, and devilish cunning, for you could see that by his eye.

But is, in fact, this the impression we have in reading the Richard of Shakspeare. Do we feel anything like disgust, as we do at that butcher-like

B

representation of him that passes for him on the stage ?   A horror at his crimes blends with the effect that we feel; but how is it qualified, how is it carried off, by the rich intellect which he displays, his resources, his wit, his buoyant spirits, his vast knowledge and insight into characters, the poetry of his part,—not an atom of all which is made perceivable in Mr C.'s way of acting it.   Nothing but his crimes, his actions, is visible; they are prominent and staring.   The murderer stands out; but where is the lofty genius, the man of vast capacity, —the profound, the witty, accomplished Richard ?

The truth is, the characters of Shakspeare are so much the objects of meditation rather than of interest or curiosity as to their actions, that while we are reading any of his great criminal characters, —Macbeth, Richard, even Iago,—we think not so much of the crimes which they commit, as of the ambition, the aspiring spirit, the intellectual activity, which prompts them to overleap these moral fences.   Barnwell is a wretched murderer; there is a certain fitness between his neck and the rope.   He is the legitimate heir to the gallows; nobody who thinks at all can think of any alleviating circumstances in his case to make him a fit object of mercy.   Or to take an instance from the higher tragedy, what else but a mere assassin is Glenalvon ?   Do we think of anything but of the crime which he commits, and the rack which he deserves ?   That is all which we really think about him.   Whereas in corresponding characters in

Shakspeare, so little do the actions comparatively affect us, that while the impulses, the inner mind in all its perverted greatness, solely seems real and is exclusively attended to, the crime is comparatively nothing. But when we see these things represented, the acts which they do are comparatively everything, their impulses nothing. The state of sublime emotion into which we are elevated by those images of night and horror which Macbeth is made to utter, that solemn prelude with which he entertains the time till the bell shall strike which is to call him to murder Duncan—when we no longer read it in a book, when we have given up that vantage ground of abstraction which reading possesses over seeing, and come to see a man in his bodily shape before our eyes actually preparing to commit a murder, if the acting be true and impressive, as I have witnessed it in Mr K—— performance of that part, the painful anxiety about the act, the natural longing to prevent it while it yet seems unperpetrated, the too close pressing semblance of reality, give a pain and an uneasiness which totally destroy all the delight which the words in the book convey, where the deed doing never presses upon us with the painful sense of presence; it rather seems to belong to history—to something past and inevitable, if it has anything to do with time at all. The sublime images, the poetry alone, is that which is present to our minds in the reading.

So to see Lear acted—to see an old man tottering

about the stage with a walking-stick, turned out of
doors by his daughters in a rainy night, has nothing
in it but what is painful and disgusting. We want
to take him into shelter and relieve him. That is
all the feeling which the acting of Lear ever produced in me. But the Lear of Shakspeare cannot
be acted. The contemptible machinery by which
they mimic the storm which he goes out in, is not
more inadequate to represent the horrors of the
real elements, than any actor can be to represent
Lear : they might more easily propose to personate
the Satan of Milton upon a stage, or one of Michael
Angelo's terrible figures. The greatness of Lear is
not in corporal dimension, but in intellectual ; the
explosions of his passions are terrible as a volcano ;
they are storms turning up and disclosing to the
bottom that sea, his mind, with all its vast riches.
It is his mind which is laid bare. This case of
flesh and blood seems too insignificant to be thought
on ; even as he himself neglects it. On the stage
we see nothing but corporal infirmities and weakness, the impotence of rage. While we read it, we
see not Lear, but we are Lear : we are in his mind,
we are sustained by a grandeur which baffles the
malice of daughters and storms. In the aberrations
of his reason we discover a mighty irregular power
of reasoning, immethodized from the ordinary purposes of life, but exerting its powers, as ' the wind
bloweth where it listeth,' at will upon the corruptions and abuses of mankind. What have looks, or
tones, to do with that sublime identification of his

age with that of the *heavens themselves,* when, in
his reproaches to them for conniving at the injustice
of his children, he reminds them that ' they themselves are old.' What gesture shall we appropriate
to this ? What has the voice or the eye to do with
such things ? But the play is beyond all art, as
the tamperings with it show: it is too hard and
stony; it must have love-scenes, and a happy
ending. It is not enough that Cordelia is a
daughter; she must shine as a lover too. Tate
has put his hook in the nostrils of this Leviathan,
for Garrick and his followers, the show-men of the
scene, to draw the mighty beast about more easily.
A happy ending!—as if the living martyrdom that
Lear had gone through—the flaying of his feelings
alive, did not make a fair dismissal from the stage
of life the only decorous thing for him. If he is to
live and be happy after, if he could sustain this
world's burden after, why all this pudder and preparation—why torment us with all this unnecessary
sympathy ? As if the childish pleasure of getting
his gilt robes and sceptre again could tempt him to
act over again his misused station!—as if, at his
years and with his experience, anything was left
but to die!

Lear is essentially impossible to be represented
on a stage. But how many dramatic personages
are there in Shakspeare, which though more
tractable and feasible (if I may so speak) than
Lear, yet from some circumstance, some adjunct
to their character, are improper to be shown to our

bodily eye! Othello read of a young Venetian
lady of the highest extraction, through the force
of love and from a sense of merit in him whom
she loved, laying aside every consideration of
kindred, and country, and colour, and wedding
with a *coal-black Moor*—(for such he is represented, in the imperfect state of knowledge respect-
ing foreign countries in those days, compared with
our own, or in compliance with popular notions,
though the Moors are now well enough known to be
by many shades less unworthy of a white woman's
fancy)—it is the perfect triumph of virtue over
accidents, of the imagination over the senses. She
sees Othello's colour in his mind. But upon the
stage, when the imagination is no longer the ruling
faculty, but we are left to our poor unassisted senses,
I appeal to every one that has seen Othello played,
whether he did not, on the contrary, sink Othello's
mind in his colour; whether he did not find something extremely revolting in the courtship and
wedded caresses of Othello and Desdemona; and
whether the actual sight of the thing did not over-
weigh all that beautiful compromise which we
make in reading, and the reason it should do is
obvious, because there is just so much reality presented to our senses as to give a perception of dis-
agreement, with not enough of belief in the internal
motives,—all that which is unseen,—to overpower
and reconcile the first and obvious perjudices.*

* The error of supposing that because Othello's colour does not offend
us in the reading, it should also not offend us in the seeing, is just such

What we see upon a stage is body and bodily action; what we are conscious of in reading is almost exclusively the mind, and its movements; and this I think may sufficiently account for the very different sort of delight with which the same play so often affects us in the reading and the seeing.

It requires little reflection to perceive, that if those characters in Shakspeare which are within the precincts of nature, have yet something in them which appeals too exclusively to the imagination, to admit of their being made objects to the senses without suffering a change and a diminution,—that still stronger the objection must lie against representing another line of characters, which Shakspeare has introduced to give a wildness and a supernatural elevation to his scenes, as if to remove them still further from that assimilation to common life in which their excellence is vulgarly supposed to consist. When we read the incantations of those terrible beings the witches in Macbeth, though some of the ingredients of their hellish composition savour of the grotesque, yet is the effect upon us other than the most serious and appalling that can be imagined? Do we not feel spell-bound as Macbeth was? Can

a fallacy as supposing that an Adam and Eve in a picture shall affect us just as they do in the poem. But in the poem we for a while have Paradisaical senses given us, which vanish when we see a man and his wife without clothes in the picture. The painters themselves feel this, as is apparent by the awkward shifts they have recourse to, to make them look not quite naked; by a sort of prophetic anachronism, antedating the invention of fig-leaves. So in the reading of the play, we see with Desdemona's eyes: in the seeing of it, we are forced to look with our own.

any mirth accompany a sense of their presence ? We might as well laugh under a consciousness of the principle of Evil himself being truly and really present with us. But attempt to bring these things on to a stage, and you turn them instantly into so many old women, that men and children are to laugh at. Contrary to the old saying, that 'seeing is believing,' the sight actually destroys the faith; and the mirth in which we indulge at their expense, when we see these creatures upon a stage, seems to be a sort of indemnification which we make to ourselves for the terror which they put us in when reading made them an object of belief, when we surrendered up our reason to the poet, as children to their nurses and their elders; and we laugh at our fears as children, who thought they saw something in the dark, triumph when the bringing in of a candle discovers the vanity of their fears. For this exposure of supernatural agents upon a stage is truly bringing in a candle to expose their own delusiveness. It is the solitary taper and the book that generates a faith in these terrors; a ghost by chandelier light, and in good company, deceives no spectators,—a ghost that can be measured by the eye, and his human dimensions made out at leisure.

The sight of a well-lighted house, and a well-dressed audience, shall arm the most nervous child against any apprehensions; as Tom Brown says of the impenetrable skin of Achilles with his impenetrable armour over it, 'Bully Dawson would have fought the Devil with such advantages.'

Much has been said, and deservedly, in reprobation of the vile mixture which Dryden has thrown
into the Tempest. Doubtless without some such
vicious alloy, the impure ears of that age would
never have sate out to hear so much innocence of
love as is contained in the sweet courtship of
Ferdinand and Miranda. But is the Tempest of
Shakspeare at all a fit subject for stage representation? It is one thing to read of an enchanter, and
to believe the wondrous tale while we are reading it;
but to have a conjuror brought before us in his con-
juring-gown, with his spirits about him, which none
but himself and some hundred of favoured spectators before the curtain are supposed to see, involved
such a quantity of the *hateful incredible*, that all
our reverence for the author cannot hinder us from
perceiving such gross attempts upon the senses to
be in the highest degree childish and inefficient.
Spirits and fairies cannot be represented; they
cannot even be painted; they can only be believed.
But the elaborate and anxious provision of scenery,
which the luxury of the age demands, in these
cases works a quite contrary effect to what is
intended. That which in comedy, or plays of
familiar life, adds so much to the life of the imitation, in plays which appeal to the higher faculties
positively destroys the illusion which it is introduced to aid. A parlour or a drawing-room,—a
library opening into a garden,—a garden with an
alcove in it,—a street, or the piazza of Covent
Garden, does well enough in a scene; we are con-

tent to give as much credit to it as it demands; or rather, we think little about it,—it is little more than reading at the top of a page, 'Scene, a Garden;' we do not imagine ourselves there, but we readily admit the imitation of familiar objects. But to think by the help of painted trees and caverns, which we know to be painted, to transport our minds to Prospero, and his island and his lonely cell;* or by the aid of a fiddle dexterously thrown in, in an interval of speaking, to make us believe that we hear those supernatural noises of which the isle was full; the Orrery Lecturer at the Haymarket might as well hope, by his musical glasses, cleverly stationed out of sight behind his apparatus, to make us believe that we do indeed hear the crystal spheres ring out that chime, which if it were to enwrap our fancy long, Milton thinks,

> 'Time would run back and fetch the age of gold,
> And speckled Vanity
> Would sicken soon and die,
> And leprous Sin would melt from earthly mould;
> Yea, Hell itself would pass away,
> And leave its dolorous mansions to the peering day.'

The Garden of Eden, with our first parents in it, is not more impossible to be shown on a stage, than the Enchanted Isle, with its no less interesting and innocent first settlers.

The subject of Scenery is closely connected with

---

* It will be said these things are done in pictures. But pictures and scenes are very different things. Painting is a world of itself, but in scene-painting there is the attempt to deceive; and there is the discordancy, never to be got over, between painted scenes and real people.

that of the Dresses, which are so anxiously attended
to on our stage. I remember the last time I saw
Macbeth played, the discrepancy I felt at the
changes of garment which he varied, the shifting
and re-shiftings, like a Romish priest at mass. The
luxury of stage improvements, and the importunity
of the public eye, require this. The coronation robe
of the Scottish monarch was fairly a counterpart
to that which our king wears when he goes to the
Parliament House, just so full and cumbersome,
and set out with ermine and pearls. And if things
must be represented, I see not what to find fault
with in this. But in reading, what robe are we
conscious of? Some dim images of royalty — a
crown and sceptre — may float before our eyes;
but who shall describe the fashion of it? Do we
see in our own mind's eye what Webb or any other
robe-maker could pattern? This is the inevitable
consequence of imitating everything, to make all
things natural. Whereas the reading of a tragedy
is a fine abstraction. It presents to the fancy just
so much of external appearances as to make us feel
that we are among flesh and blood, while by far the
greater and better part of our imagination is employed upon the thoughts and internal machinery
of the character. But in acting—scenery, dress,
the most contemptible things, call upon us to judge
of their naturalness.

Perhaps it would be no bad similitude to liken
the pleasure which we take in seeing one of these
fine plays acted, compared with that quiet delight

which we find in the reading of it, to the different
feelings with which a reviewer, and a man that is
not a reviewer, reads a fine poem. The accursed
critical habit—the being called upon to judge and
pronounce, must make it quite a different thing to
the two former. In seeing these plays acted, we
are affected just as judges. When Hamlet compares
the pictures of Gertrude's first and second husband,
who wants to see the pictures? But in the acting
a miniature must be lugged out; which we know
not to be the picture, but only to show how finely
a miniature may be represented. This showing of
everything levels all things ; it makes tricks, bows,
and curtseys of importance. Mrs S—— never got
more fame by anything than by the manner in
which she dismisses the guests in the banquet scene
in Macbeth: it is as much remembered as any of
her thrilling tones or impressive looks. But does
such a trifle as this enter into the imaginations of
the readers of that wild and wonderful scene ?
Does not the mind dismiss the feasters as rapidly
as it can ? Does it care about the gracefulness of
doing it ? But by acting, and judging of acting, all
these non-essentials are raised into an importance,
injurious to the main interests of the play.

I have confined my observations to the tragic
parts of Shakspeare. It would be no very difficult
task to extend the inquiry to his comedies; and to
show why Falstaff, Shallow, Sir Hugh Evans, and
the rest, are equally incompatible with stage repre-

sentation. The length to which this essay has run
will make it, I am afraid, sufficiently distasteful to
the amateurs of the theatre, without going any
deeper into the subject at present.

BARRENNESS OF THE IMAGINATIVE FACULTY IN THE PRODUCTIONS OF MODERN ART

HOGARTH excepted, can we produce any one painter within the last fifty years, or since the humour of exhibiting began, that has treated a story *imaginatively?*—By this we mean, upon whom his subject has so acted, that it has seemed to direct *him*, not to be arranged by him?—Any upon whom its leading or collateral points have impressed themselves so tyrannically that he dared not treat it otherwise, lest he should falsify a revelation?—Any that has imparted to his compositions, not merely so much truth as is enough to convey a story with clearness, but that individualizing property, which should keep the subject so treated distinct in feature from

every other subject, however similar, and to common apprehensions almost identical; so that we
might say, this and this part could have found an
appropriate place in no other picture in the world
but this? Is there anything in modern art—we
would not demand that it should be equal—but in
any way analogous to what Titian has effected, in
that wonderful bringing together of two times in
the ' Ariadne,' in the National Gallery ? Precipitous,
with his reeling satyr rout about him, re-peopling
and re-illumining suddenly the waste places, drunk
with a new fury beyond the grape, Bacchus, born
in fire, fire-like flings himself at the Cretan. This
is the time present. With this telling of the story,
an artist, and no ordinary one, might remain richly
proud. Guido, in his harmonious version of it, saw
no further. But from the depths of the imaginative
spirit Titian has recalled past time, and laid it con-
tributory with the present to one simultaneous
effect. With the desert all ringing with the mad
cymbals of his followers, made lucid with the
presence and new offers of a god—as if unconscious
of Bacchus, or but idly casting her eyes as upon some
unconcerning pageant, her soul undistracted from
Theseus—Ariadne is still pacing the solitary shore
in as much heart silence, and in almost the same
local solitude, with which she awoke at daybreak
to catch the forlorn last glances of the sail that bore
away the Athenian.

Here are two points miraculously co-uniting;
fierce society, with the feeling of solitude still

absolute ; noon-day revelations, with the accidents
of the dull gray dawn unquenched and lingering ;
the *present* Bacchus, with the *past* Ariadne ; two
stories, with double Time ; separate, and harmonis-
ing. Had the artist made the woman one shade
less indifferent to the god ; still more, had she expressed a rapture at his advent, where would have
been the story of the mighty desolation of the heart
previous ? merged in the insipid accident of a
flattering offer met with a welcome acceptance.
The broken heart for Theseus was not lightly to be
pieced up by a god.

We have before us a fine rough print, from a picture by Raphael in the Vatican. It is the Presentation of the new-born Eve to Adam by the Almighty.
A fairer mother of mankind we might imagine,
and a goodlier sire perhaps of men since born. But
these are matters subordinate to the conception of
the *situation* displayed in this extraordinary production. A tolerably modern artist would have
been satisfied with tempering certain raptures of
connubial anticipation with a suitable acknowledg-
ment to the Giver of the blessing, in the countenance
of the first bridegroom ; something like the divided
attention of the child (Adam was here a child-man)
between the given toy and the mother who had just
blest it with the bauble. This is the obvious, the
first-sight view, the superficial. An artist of a
higher grade, considering the awful presence they
were in, would have taken care to subtract something from the expression of the more human

passion, and to heighten the more spiritual one.
This would be as much as an exhibition-goer, from
the opening of Somerset House, to last year's
show, has been encouraged to look for. It is
obvious to hint at a lower expression yet, in a
picture that, for respects of drawing and colouring,
might be deemed not wholly inadmissible within
these art-fostering walls, in which the raptures
should be as ninety-nine, the gratitude as one, or
perhaps zero! By neither the one passion nor the
other has Raphael expounded the situation of
Adam. Singly upon his brow sits the absorbing
sense of wonder at the created miracle. The
moment is seized by the intuitive artist, perhaps
not self-conscious of his art, in which neither of the
conflicting emotions (a moment how abstracted!)
has had time to spring up, or to battle for indecorous
mastery. We have seen a landscape of a justly
admired neoteric, in which he aimed at delineating
a fiction, one of the most severely beautiful in
antiquity,—the Gardens of the Hesperides. To do
Mr—— justice, he had painted a laudable orchard,
with fitting seclusion, and a veritable dragon, (of
which a Polypheme, by Poussin, is somehow a fac-
simile for the situation), looking over into the
world shut out backwards, so that none but a 'still-
climbing Hercules' could hope to catch a peep at
the admired Ternary of Recluses. No conventual
porter could keep his eyes better than this custos
with the 'lidless eyes.' He not only sees that none
do intrude into that privacy, but, as clear as day-

C

light, that none but *Hercules aut Diabolus* by any
manner of means *can.* So far all is well. We have
absolute solitude here or nowhere. *Ab extra,* the
damsels are snug enough. But here the artist's
courage seems to have failed him. He began to
pity his pretty charge, and to comfort the irksome-
ness has peopled their solitude with a bevy of fair
attendants, maids of honour or ladies of the bed-
chamber, according to the approved etiquette at a
Court of the nineteenth century; giving to the
whole scene the air of a *fête champêtre* if we will
but excuse the absence of the gentlemen. This is
well and Watteauish. But what is become of the
solitary mystery—the

> Daughters there,
> That sing around the golden tree ?

This is not the way in which Poussin would have
treated this subject.

The paintings, or rather the stupendous architectural designs, of a modern artist, have been urged
as objections to the theory of our motto. They are
of a character, we confess, to stagger it. His towered
structures are of the highest order of the material
sublime. Whether they were dreams, or transcripts
of some elder workmanship—Assyrian ruins old—
restored by this mighty artist, they satisfy our most
stretched and craving conceptions of the glories of
the antique world. It is a pity that they were ever
peopled. On that side the imagination of the artist
halts, and appears defective. Let us examine the

point of the story in the 'Belshazzar's Feast.' We
will introduce it by an apposite anecdote.

The Court historians of the day record, that at
the first dinner given by the late King (then Prince
Regent) at the Pavilion, the following characteristic
frolic was played off. The guests were select and
admiring; the banquet was profuse and admirable ;
the lights lustrous and oriental ; the eye was perfectly dazzled with the display of plate, among
which the great gold salt-cellar, brought from the
regalia in the Tower for this especial purpose, (itself
a tower!) stood conspicuous for its magnitude.
And now the Rev ＊＊＊＊, the then admired Court
Chaplain, was proceeding with the grace, when, at
a signal given, the lights were suddenly overcast,
and a huge transparency was discovered, in which
glittered in gold letters—

' BRIGHTON !— EARTHQUAKE !— SWALLOW
UP ALIVE!'

Imagine the confusion of the guests; the Georges
and garters, jewels, bracelets, moulted upon the
occasion!—the fans dropped, and picked up the
next morning by the sly Court pages !—Mrs Fitz-
what's-her-name fainting and the Countess of......
holding the smelling-bottle, till the good-humoured
Prince caused harmony to be restored by calling in
fresh candles, and declaring that the whole was
nothing but a pantomime *hoax*, got up by the ingenious Mr Farley, of Covent Garden, from hints

which his Royal Highness himself had furnished !
Then imagine the infinite applause that followed,
the mutual rallyings of the assembled galaxy, the
declarations that 'they were not much frightened!'

The point of time in the picture exactly answers
to the appearance of the transparency in the anecdote. The huddle, the flutter, the bustle, the escape,
the alarm, and the mock alarm; the prettinesses
heightened by consternation; the courtier's fear
which was flattery; and the lady's which was affectation; all that we may conceive to have taken
place in a mob of Brighton courtiers, sympathizing
with the well-acted surprise of their sovereign; all
this, and no more, is exhibited by the well-dressed
lords and ladies in the Hall of Belus. Just this
sort of consternation we have seen among a flock
of disquieted wild geese at the report only of a gun
having gone off!

But is this vulgar fright, this mere animal anxiety
for the preservation of their persons,—such as we
have witnessed at a theatre when a slight alarm of
fire has been given—an adequate exponent of a
supernatural terror? the way in which the finger
of God, writing judgments, would have been met
by the withered conscience? There is a human
fear, and a divine fear. The one is disturbed, restless, and bent upon escape. The other is bowed
down, effortless, passive. When the spirit appeared
before Eliphaz in the visions of the night, and the
hair of his flesh stood up, was it in the thoughts of
the Temanite to ring the bell of his chamber, or to

call up the servants? But let us see in the text what there is to justify all this huddle of vulgar consternation.

From the words of Daniel it appears that Belshazzar had made a great feast to a thousand of his lords, and drank wine before the thousand. The golden and silver vessels are gorgeously enumerated, with the princes, the king's concubines, and his wives. Then follows—

'In the same hour came forth fingers of a man's hand, and wrote over against the candlestick upon the plaister of the wall of the king's palace; and the king saw the part of the hand that wrote. Then the king's countenance was changed, and his thoughts troubled him so that the joints of his loins were loosed, and his knees smote one against another.'

This is the plain text. By no hint can it be otherwise inferred, but that the appearance was solely confined to the fancy of Belshazzar, that his single brain was troubled. Not a word is spoken of its being seen by any one else there present, not even by the queen herself, who merely undertakes for the interpretation of the phenomenon, as related to her, doubtless, by her husband. The lords are simply said to be astonished; *i.e.*, at the trouble and the change of countenance in their sovereign. Even the prophet does not appear to have seen the scroll which the king saw. He recalls it only, as Joseph did the dream to the king of Egypt. 'Then was the part of the hand sent from him (the Lord);

and this writing was written.' He speaks of the phantasm as past.

Then what becomes of this needless multiplication of the miracle? this message to a royal conscience, singly expressed, for it was said, 'Thy kingdom is divided,' simultaneously impressed upon the fancies of a thousand courtiers, who were implied in it neither directly nor grammatically?

But admitting the artist's own version of the story, and that the sight was seen also by the thousand courtiers—let it have been visible to all Babylon—as the knees of Belshazzar were shaken, and his countenance troubled, even so would the knees of every man in Babylon, and their countenances, as of an individual man, have been troubled; bowed, bent down, so would they have remained, stupor-fixed, with no thought of struggling with that inevitable judgment.

Not all that is optically possible to be seen is to be shown in every picture. The eye delightedly dwells upon the brilliant individualities in a 'Marriage at Cana,' by Veronese or Titian, to the very texture and colour of the wedding garments, the ring glittering upon the bride's finger, the metal and fashion of the wine-pots; for at such seasons there is leisure and luxury to be curious. But in a 'Day of Judgment,' or in a 'day of lesser horrors yet divine,' as at the impious feast of Belshazzar, the eye should see, as the actual eye of an agent or patient in the immediate scene would see, only in masses and indistinction. Not only the female attire and jewelry exposed to the critical eye of fashion, as minutely as the dresses in a Lady's Magazine, in the criticised picture,—but perhaps the curiosities of anatomical science, and studied diversities of posture,—in the falling angels and sinners of Michael Angelo have no business in their great subjects. There was no leisure for them.

By a wise falsification, the great masters of painting got at their true conclusions, by not showing the actual appearances; that is, not all that was to be seen at any given moment by an indifferent eye but only what the eye might be supposed to see in the doing or suffering of some portentous action. Suppose the moment of the swallowing up of Pompeii. There they were to be seen—houses, columns, architectural proportions, differences of public and private buildings, men and women at their standing occupations, the diversified thousand postures, attitudes, dresses, in some confusion truly, but physically they were visible. But what eye saw them at that eclipsing moment, which reduces confusion to a kind of unity, and when the senses are upturned from their proprieties, when sight and hearing are a feeling only? A thousand years have passed, and we are at leisure to contemplate the weaver fixed standing at his shuttle, the baker at his oven, and to turn over with antiquarian coolness the pots and pans of Pompeii.

'Sun, stand thou still upon Gibeon; and thou Moon, in the valley of Ajalon.' Who, in reading this magnificent Hebraism, in his conception sees aught but the heroic son of Nun, with the outstretched arm, and the greater and lesser light obsequious? Doubtless there were to be seen hill and dale, and chariots and horsemen, on open plain, or winding by secret defiles, and all the circumstances and stratagems of war. But whose eyes would have been conscious of this array at the interposition of the synchronical miracle ? Yet in the picture of this subject by the artist of the ‘Belshazzar’s Feast’ (no ignoble work either) the marshalling and landscape of the war is everything, the miracle sinks into an anecdote of the day ; and the eye may ‘dart through rank and file traverse’ for some minutes, before it shall discover, among his armed followers, *which is Joshua !* Not modern art alone, but ancient, where only it is to be found if anywhere, can be detected erring, from defect of this imaginative faculty. The world has nothing to show of the preternatural in painting, transcending the figure of Lazarus bursting his grave-clothes, in the great picture at Angerstein’s. It seems a thing between two beings. A ghastly horror at itself struggles with newly apprehending gratitude at second life bestowed. It cannot forget that it was a ghost. It has hardly felt that it is a body. It has to tell of the world of spirits. Was it from a feeling, that the crowd of half-impassioned by-standers, and the still more irrelevant herd of passers-by at a distance, who have not heard or but faintly have been told of the passing miracle, admirable as they are in design and hue, (for it is a glorified work,) do not respond adequately, to the action,

that the single figure of Lazarus has been attributed
to Michael Angelo, and the mighty Sebastian un-
fairly robbed of the fame of the greater half of the
interest ? Now that there were not indifferent passers-by within actual scope of the eyes of those present at the miracle, to whom the sound of it had but
faintly, or not at all, reached, it would be hardihood
to deny ; but would they see them ? or can the mind
in the conception of it admit of such unconcerning
objects? can it think of them at all? or what associat-
ing league to the imagination can there be between
the seers and the seers not of a presential miracle ?

Were an artist to paint upon demand a picture
of a Dryad, we will ask whether, in the present low
state of expectation, the patron would not (or ought
not) be fully satisfied with a beautiful naked figure
recumbent under wide stretched oaks? Disseat
those woods and place the same figure among
fountains and falls of pellucid water, and you have
a Naiad! Not so in a rough print we have seen,
after Julio Romano, we think (for it is long since)
there, by no process, with mere change of scene,
could the figure have reciprocated characters. Long,
grotesque, fantastic, yet with a grace of her own,
beautiful in convolution and distortion, linked to
her connatural tree, cotwisting with its limbs her
own, till both seemed either (these, animated
branches ; those disanimated members; yet the
animal and vegetable lives sufficiently kept distinct,) *his* Dryad lay—an approximation of two
natures, which to conceive, it must be seen.

analogous to, not the same with, the delicacies of
Ovidian transformations.

To the lowest subjects, and to a superficial com-
prehension the most barren, the Great Masters gave
loftiness and fruitfulness. The large eye of genius
saw in the meanness of present objects their capa-
bilities of treatment from their relations to some
grand Past or Future. How has Raphael (we must
still linger about the Vatican) treated the humble
craft of the ship-builder, in *his* ' Building of the
Ark?' It is in that scriptural series to which we have
referred, and which, judging from some fine rough
old graphic sketches of them which we possess,
seem to be of a higher and more poetic grade than
even the cartoons. The dim of sight are the timid
and the shrinking. There is a cowardice in modern
art. As the Frenchman, of whom Coleridge's friend
made the prophetic guess at Rome, from the beard
and horns of the Moses of Michael Angelo collected
no inferences beyond that of a He Goat and a
Cornuto ; so from this subject, of mere mechanic
promise, it would instinctively turn away, as from
one incapable of investiture with any grandeur.
The dockyards at Woolwich would object derogatory
associations. The depôt at Chatham would be the
mote and the beam in its intellectual eye. But not
to the nautical preparations in the ship-yards of
Civita Vecchia did Raphael look for instructions
when he imagined the building of the vessel that
was to be conservatory of the wrecks of the species
of drowned mankind. In the intensity of the

action he keeps ever out of sight the meanness of
the operation. There is the Patriarch, in calm fore-
thought, and with holy prescience, giving directions.
And there are his agents—the solitary but sufficient
Three—hewing, sawing, every one with the might
and earnestness of a Demiurgus; under some instinctive rather than technical guidance! giant-
muscled; every one a Hercules, or liker to those
Vulcanian Three, that in sounding caverns under
Mongibello wrought in fire—Brontes and black
Steropes and Pyracmon. So work the workmen
that should repair a world!

Artists again err in the confounding of *poetic*
with *pictorial subjects*. In the latter, the exterior
accidents are nearly everything, the unseen qualities
as nothing. Othello's colour—the infirmities and
corpulence of a Sir John Falstaff—do they haunt
us perpetually in the reading? or are they obtruded
upon our conceptions one time for ninety-nine that
we are lost in admiration at the respective moral or
intellectual attributes of the character? But in a
picture Othello is *always* a Blackamoor; and the
other only Plump Jack. Deeply corporealized, and
enchained hopelessly in the grovelling fetters of
externality, must be the mind, to which, in its better
moments, the image of the high-souled, high-
intelligenced Quixote (the errant Star of Knight-
hood, made more tender by eclipse) has never presented itself divested from the unhallowed accompaniment of a Sancho, or a rabblement at the heels
of Rosinante. That man has read his book by

halves; he has laughed, mistaking his author's purport, which was tears. The artist that pictures Quixote (and it is in this degrading point that he is every season held up at our Exhibitions) in the shallow hope of exciting mirth, would have joined the rabble at the heels of his starved steed. We wish not to see *that* counterfeited which we would not have wished to see in the reality. Conscious of the heroic inside of the noble Quixote, who, on hearing that his withered person was passing, would have stepped over his threshold to gaze upon his forlorn habiliments, and the 'strange bed-fellows which misery brings a man acquainted with?' Shade of Cervantes; who in thy Second Part could put into the mouth of thy Quixote those high aspirations of a super-chivalrous gallantry, where he replies to one of the shepherdesses, apprehensive that he would spoil their pretty net-works, and inviting him to be a guest with them, in accents like these: 'Truly, fairest Lady, Actæon was not more astonished when he saw Diana bathing herself at the fountain than I have been in beholding your beauty: I commend the manner of your pastime, and thank you for your kind offers; and, if I may serve you, so I may be sure you will be obeyed, you may command me; for my profession is this—To show myself thankful, and a doer of good to all sorts of people, especially of the rank that your person shows you to be; and if those nets, as they take up but a little piece of ground, should take up the whole world, I would seek out new worlds to pass through, rather than

break them; and (he adds) that you may give
credit to this my exaggeration, behold at least
he that promiseth you this, is Don Quixote de la
Mancha, if haply this name hath come to your
hearing.' Illustrious Romancer! were the 'fine
frenzies,' which possessed the brain of thy own
Quixote, a fit subject, as in this Second Part, to be
exposed to the jeers of Duennas and Serving men;
to be monstered, and shown up at the heartless
banquets of great men? Was that pitiable infirmity, which in thy First Part misleads him,
always from within, into half-ludicrous, but more
than half-compassionable and admirable errors, not
infliction enough from heaven, that men by studied
artifices must devise and practise upon the humour,
to inflame where they should soothe it? Why,
Goneril would have blushed to practise upon the
abdicated king at this rate, and the she-wolf Regan
not have endured to play the pranks upon his fled
wits which thou hast made thy Quixote suffer in
Duchesses' halls and at the hands of that unworthy
nobleman.*

In the First Adventures, even, it needed all the
art of the most consummate artist in the Book way
that the world hath yet seen, to keep up in the
mind of the reader the heroic attributes of the
character without relaxing; so as absolutely that
they shall suffer no alloy from the debasing fellow-
ship of the clown. If it ever obtrudes itself as

---

* Yet from this Second Part our cried-up pictures are mostly
selected; the waiting women with beards, &c.

a disharmony, are we inclined to laugh ; or not, rather, to indulge a contrary emotion ?   Cervantes, stung perchance by the relish with which *his* Reading Public had received the fooleries of the man, more to their palates than the generosities of the masters, in the sequel let his pen run riot, lost the harmony and the balance, and sacrificed a great idea to the taste of his contemporaries.   We know that in the present day the knight has fewer admirers than the squire.   Anticipating what did actually happen to him—as afterwards it did to his scarce inferior follower, the author of ' Guzman de Alfarache '—that some less knowing hand would prevent him by a spurious Second Part ; and judging that it would be easier for his competitor to out-bid him in the comicalities than in the *romance* of his work, he abandoned his Knight, and has fairly set up the Squire for his hero.   For what else has he unsealed the eyes of Sancho ? and why, instead of that twilight state of semi-insanity (the madness at second-hand—the contagion caught from a stronger mind infected—that war between native cunning and hereditary deference, with which he has hitherto accompanied his master—two for a pair almost) does he substitute a downright knave, with open eyes, for his own ends only following a confessed madman ; and offering at one time to lay, if not actually laying, hands upon him !   From the moment that Sancho loses his reverence, Don Quixote is become a treatable lunatic.   Our artists handle him accordingly.

A PLAY is said to be well or ill acted in proportion to the scenical illusion produced. Whether such illusion can in any case be perfect, is not the question. The nearest approach to it, we are told, is when the actor appears wholly unconscious of the presence of spectators. In tragedy—in all which is to affect the feelings—this undivided attention to his stage business seems indispensable. Yet it is, in fact, dispensed with every day by our cleverest tragedians; and while these references to an audience, in the shape of rant or sentiment, are not too frequent or palpable, a sufficient quantity of illusion for the purposes of dramatic interest may be said to be produced in spite of them. But, tragedy apart, it may be inquired whether,

in certain characters in comedy, especially those
which are a little extravagant, or which involve
some notion repugnant to the moral sense, it is not
a proof of the highest skill in the comedian when,
without absolutely appealing to an audience, he
keeps up a tacit understanding with them; and
makes them, unconsciously to themselves, a party
in the scene. The utmost nicety is required in the
mode of doing this; but we speak only of the
great artists in the profession.

The most mortifying infirmity in human nature,
to feel in ourselves, or to contemplate in another, is
perhaps cowardice. To see a coward *done to the
life* upon a stage would produce anything but mirth.
Yet we most of us remember Jack Bannister's
cowards. Could anything be more agreeable, more
pleasant? We loved the rogues. How was this
effected but by the exquisite art of the actor in a
perpetual sub-insinuation to us, the spectators, even
in the extremity of the shaking fit, that he was not
half such a coward as we took him for? We saw
all the common symptoms of the malady upon him,
—the quivering lip, the cowering knees, the teeth
chattering,—and could have sworn 'that man was
frightened.' But we forgot all the while—or kept
it almost a secret to ourselves—that he never once
lost his self-possession; that he let out, by a
thousand droll looks and gestures—meant at *us*,
and not at all supposed to be visible to his fellows
in the scene—that his confidence in his own resources had never once deserted him. Was this a

genuine picture of a coward?—or not rather a likeness, which the clever artist contrived to palm upon us instead of an original; while we secretly connived at the delusion for the purpose of greater pleasure than a more genuine counterfeiting of the imbecility, helplessness, and utter self-desertion, which we know to be concomitants of cowardice in real life, could have given us?

Why are misers so hateful in the world, and so endurable on the stage, but because the skilful actor, by a sort of sub-reference, rather than direct appeal to us, disarms the character of a great deal of its odiousness, by seeming to engage our compassion for the insecure tenure by which he holds his money-bags and parchments? By this subtle vent half of the hatefulness of the character—the self-closeness with which in real life it coils itself up from the sympathies of men—evaporates. The miser becomes sympathetic; *i.e.* is no genuine miser. Here again a diverting likeness is substituted for a very disagreeable reality.

Spleen, irritability—the pitiable infirmities of old men, which produce only pain to behold in the realities—counterfeited upon a stage, divert not altogether for the comic appendages to them, but in part from an inner conviction that they are *being acted* before us; that a likeness only is going on, and not the thing itself. They please by being done under the life, or beside it; not *to the life.* When Gattie acts an old man, is he angry indeed? or only a pleasant counterfeit, just enough of a

D

likeness to recognise, without pressing upon us the
uneasy sense of a reality ?

Comedians, paradoxical as it may seem, may be
too natural. It was the case with a late actor.
Nothing could be more earnest or true than the
manner of Mr. Emery; this told excellently in his
Tyke, and characters of a tragic cast. But when
he carried the same rigid exclusiveness of attention
to the stage business, and wilful blindness and oblivion of everything before the curtain into his
comedy, it produced a harsh and dissonant effect.
It was out of keeping with the rest of the *Personæ Dramatis.* There was as little link between
him and them, as betwixt himself and the audience.
He was a third estate, dry, repulsive, and unsocial
to all. Individually considered, his execution was
masterly. But comedy is not this unbending thing;
for this reason, that the same degree of credibility
is not required of it as to serious scenes. The
degrees of credibility demanded to the two things,
may be illustrated by the different sort of truth
which we expect when a man tells us a mournful
or a merry story. If we suspect the former
of falsehood in any one tittle, we reject it altogether. Our tears refuse to flow at a suspected
imposition. But the teller of a mirthful tale
has latitude allowed him. We are content with
less than absolute truth. 'Tis the same with
dramatic illusion. We confess we love in comedy
to see an audience naturalized behind the scenes,
taken into the interest of the drama, welcomed as

bystanders however. There is something ungracious in a comic actor holding himself aloof from all participation or concern with those who are come to be diverted by him. Macbeth must see the dagger, and no ear but his own be told of it; but an old fool in farce may think he *sees something*, and by conscious words and looks express it, as plainly as he can speak, to pit, box, and gallery. When an impertinent in tragedy—an Osric, for instance —breaks in upon the serious passions of the scene, we approve of the contempt with which he is treated. But when the pleasant impertinent of com'edy, in a piece purely meant to give delight, and raise mirth out of whimsical perplexities, worries the studious man with taking up his leisure, or making his house his home, the same sort of contempt expressed (however *natural*) would destroy the balance of delight in the spectators. To make the intrusion comic, the actor who plays the annoyed man must a little desert nature; he must, in short, be thinking of the audience, and express only so much dissatisfaction and peevishness as is consistent with the pleasure of comedy. In other words, his perplexity must seem half put on. If he repel the intruder with the sober set face of a man in earnest, and more especially if he deliver his expostulations in a tone which in the world must necessarily provoke a duel, his real-life manner will destroy the whimsical and purely dramatic existence of the other character (which to render it comic demands an antagonist comicality on the part of the character opposed to it) and convert what was meant for mirth, rather than belief, into a downright piece of impertinence indeed, which would raise no diversion in us, but rather stir pain, to see inflicted in earnest upon any unworthy person. A very judicious actor (in most of his parts) seems to have fallen into an error of this sort in his playing with Mr Wrench in the farce of *Free and Easy*.

Many instances would be tedious: these may suffice to show that comic acting, at least, does not always demand from the performer that strict abstraction from all reference to an audience which is exacted of it; but that in some cases a sort of compromise may take place, and all the purposes of dramatic delight be attained by a judicious understanding, not too openly announced, between the ladies and gentlemen on both sides of the curtain.

THE casual sight of an old Play Bill, which I picked up the other day—I knew not by what chance it was preserved so long—tempts me to call to mind a few of the Players who make the principal figure in it. It presents the cast of parts in the *Twelfth Night*, at the old Drury Lane Theatre two-and-thirty years ago. There is something very touching in these old remembrances. They make us think how we *once used to read* a Play Bill—not as now peradventure, singling out a favourite performer, and casting a negligent eye over the rest; but spelling out every name, down to the very mutes and servants of the scene; when it was a matter of no small moment to us whether Whitfield or Packer took the part of Fabian; when Benson, and

Burton, and Phillimore—names of small account—
had an importance beyond what we can be content
to attribute now to the time's best actors. 'Orsino,
by Mr Barrymore.' What a full Shakspearian
sound it carries! how fresh to memory arise the
image and the manner of the gentle actor !

Those who have only seen Mrs Jordan within the
last ten or fifteen years can have no adequate notion
of her performance of such parts as Ophelia;
Helena in *All's Well that Ends Well;* and Viola in
this play. Her voice had latterly acquired a
coarseness, which suited well enough with her Nells
and Hoydens, but in those days it sank, with her
steady, melting eye, into the heart. Her joyous
parts, in which her memory now chiefly lives, in
her youth were outdone by her plaintive ones.
There is no giving an account how she delivered
the disguised story of her love for Orsino. It was
no set speech, that she had foreseen, so as to weave
it into an harmonious period, line necessarily following line, to make up the music—yet I have heard
it so spoken, or rather *read*, not without its grace
and beauty—but, when she had declared her sister's
history to be a 'blank,' and that she 'never told
love,' there was a pause, as if the story had
ended—and then the image of the 'worm in the
bud,' came up as a new suggestion—and the
heightened image of 'Patience' still followed after
that, as by some growing (and not mechanical) process, thought springing up after thought, I would

almost say, as they were watered by her tears. So
in those fine lines—

Right loyal cantos of contemned love —
Hollow your name to the reverberate hills—

there was no preparation made in the foregoing
image for that which was to follow. She used no
rhetoric in her passion ; or it was Nature's own
rhetoric, most legitimate then, when it seemed
altogether without rule or law.

Mrs Powel (now Mrs Renard), then in the pride
of her beauty, made an admirable Olivia. She
was particularly excellent in her unbending scenes
in conversation with the Clown. I have seen some
Olivias—and those very sensible actresses too—who
in these interlocutions have seemed to set their wits
at the jester, and to vie conceits with him in downright emulation. But she used him for her sport,
like what he was, to trifle a leisure sentence or two
with, and then to be dismissed, and she to be the
Great Lady still. She touched the imperious fantastic humour of the character with nicety. Her
fine spacious person filled the scene.

The part of Malvolio has, in my judgment, been
so often misunderstood, and the *general merits* of
the actor, who then played it, so unduly appreciated,
that I shall hope for pardon if I am a little prolix
upon these points.

Of all the actors who flourished in my time—a
melancholy phase if taken aright, reader—Bensley

had most of the swell of soul, was greatest in the
delivery of heroic conceptions, the emotions conse-
quent upon the presentment of a great idea to the
fancy. He had the true poetical enthusiasm—the
rarest faculty among players. None that I remember possessed even a portion of that fine madness
which he threw out in Hotspur's famous rant about
glory, or the transports of the Venetian incendiary
at the vision of the fired city. His voice had the
dissonance, and at times the inspiriting effect, of the
trumpet. His gait was uncouth and stiff, but no
way embarrassed by affectation; and the thorough-
bred gentleman was uppermost in every movement. He seized the moment of passion with
greatest truth; like a faithful clock, never striking before the time; never anticipating or leading
you to anticipate. He was totally destitute of
trick and artifice. He seemed come upon the
stage to do the poet's message simply, and he did
it with as genuine fidelity as the nuncios in Homer
deliver the errands of the gods. He let the passion or the sentiment do its own work without
prop or bolstering. He would have scorned to
mountebank it; and betrayed none of that *cleverness*
which is the bane of serious acting. For this reason,
his Iago was the only endurable one which I remember to have seen. No spectator, from his action,
could divine more of his artifice than Othello was
supposed to do. His confessions in soliloquy alone
put you in possession of the mystery. There were
no by-intimations to make the audience fancy their

own discernment so much greater than that of the
Moor—who commonly stands like a great helpless
mark, set up for mine Ancient, and a quantity of
barren spectators, to shoot their bolts at. The Iago
of Bensley did not go to work so grossly. There was
a triumphant tone about the character, natural to a
general consciousness of power; but none of that
petty vanity which chuckles and cannot contain
itself upon any little successful stroke of its knavery
—as is common with your small villains, and green
probationers in mischief. It did not clap or crow
before its time. It was not a man setting his wits at
a child, and winking all the while at other children,
who are mightily pleased at being let into the secret;
but a consummate villain entrapping a noble nature
into toils, against which no discernment was available, where the manner was as fathomless as the
purpose seemed dark, and without motive. The part
of Malvolio, in the *Twelfth Night*, was performed by
Bensley with a richness and a dignity of which (to
judge from some recent castings of that character)
the very tradition must be worn out from the stage.
No manager in those days would have dreamed of
giving it to Mr Baddeley or Mr Parsons; when
Bensley was occasionally absent from the theatre,
John Kemble thought it no derogation to succeed
to the part. Malvolio is not essentially ludicrous.
He becomes comic but by accident. He is cold,
austere, repelling; but dignified, consistent, and,
for what appears, rather of an over-stretched
morality. Maria describes him as a sort of

Puritan; and he might have worn his gold
chain with honour in one of our old round-head
families, in the service of a Lambert or a Lady
Fairfax. But his morality and his manners are
misplaced in Illyria. He is opposed to the proper
levities of the piece, and falls in the unequal
contest. Still his pride, or his gravity, (call it
which you will), is inherent, and native to the
man, not mock or affected, which latter only are
the fit objects to excite laughter. His quality is
at the best unlovely, but neither buffoon nor
contemptible. His bearing is lofty, a little above
his station, but probably not much above his
deserts. We see no reason why he should not
have been brave, honourable, accomplished. His
careless committal of the ring to the ground (which
he was commissioned to restore to Cesario)
bespeaks a generosity of birth and feeling.
His dialect on all occasions is that of a gentleman and a man of education. We must not confound him with the eternal old, low steward of
comedy. He is master of the household to a
great princess; a dignity probably conferred upon
him for other respects than age or length of service.
Olivia, at the first indication of his supposed madness, declares that she 'would not have him mis-
carry for half of her dowry.' Does this look as
if the character was meant to appear little or insignificant? Once, indeed, she accuses him to his
face—of what?—of being 'sick of self-love,'—but
with a gentleness and considerateness which could

not have been if she had not thought that this particular infirmity shaded some virtues. His rebuke to the knight and the sottish revellers is sensible and spirited; and when we take into consideration the unprotected condition of his mistress, and the strict regard with which her state of real or dissembled mourning would draw the eyes of the world upon her house affairs, Malvolio might feel the honour of the family in some sort in his keeping, as it appears not that Olivia had any more brothers or kinsmen to look to it—for Sir Toby had dropped all such nice respects at the buttery-hatch. That Malvolio was meant to be represented as possessing estimable qualities, the expression of the Duke in his anxiety to have him reconciled, almost infers: 'Pursue him, and entreat him to a peace.' Even in his abused state of chains and darkness, a sort of greatness seems never to desert him. He argues highly and well with the supposed Sir Topas, and philosophises gallantly upon his straw.* There must have been some shadow of worth about the man; he must have been something more than a mere vapour—a thing of straw, or Jack in office— before Fabian and Maria could have ventured sending him upon a courting errand to Olivia. There was some consonancy (as he would say) in the undertaking, or the jest would have been too bold even for that house of misrule.

Clown. What is the opinion of Pythagorus concerning wild fowl?
Mal. That the soul of our grandam might haply inhabit a bird.
Clown. What thinkest though of his opinion?
Mal. I think nobly of the soul, and no way approve his opinion.

Bensley, accordingly threw over the part an air
of Spanish loftiness. He looked, spake, and moved
like an old Castilian. He was starch, spruce,
opinionated, but his superstructure of pride seemed
bottomed upon a sense of worth. There was something in it beyond the coxcomb. It was big and
swelling, but you could not be sure that it was
hollow. You might wish to see it taken down, but
you felt that it was upon an elevation. He was
magnificent from the outset; but when the decent
sobrieties of the character began to give way,
and the poison of self-love, in his conceit of the
Countess's affection, gradually to work, you would
have thought that the hero of La Mancha in
person stood before you. How he went smiling
to himself! With what ineffable carelessness would
he twirl his gold chain! What a dream it was!
You were infected with the illusion, and did
not wish that it should be removed. You had
no room for laughter. If an unseasonable reflection of morality obtruded itself, it was a deep
sense of the pitiable infirmity of man's nature,
that can lay him open to such frenzies; but, in
truth, you rather admired than pitied the lunacy
while it lasted; you felt that an hour of such
mistake was worth an age with the eyes open.
Who would not wish to live but for a day in
the conceit of such a lady's love as Olivia? Why,
the Duke would have given his principality but
for a quarter of a minute, sleeping or waking,
to have been so deluded. The man seemed to

tread upon air, to taste manna, to walk with his head in the cloud, to mate Hyperion. Oh, shake not the castles of his pride; endure yet for a season bright moments of confidence; 'stand still, ye watches of the element,' that Malvolio may be still in fancy fair Olivia's lord!—but fate and retribution say 'No.' I hear the mis- chievous titter of Maria—the witty taunts of Sir Toby—the still more insupportable triumph of the foolish knight—the counterfeit Sir Topas is un- masked—and 'thus the whirligig of time,' as the true clown hath it, 'brings in his revenges.' I con- fess that I never saw the catastrophe of this character while Bensley played it, without a kind of tragic interest. There was good foolery too. Few now remember Dodd. What an Aguecheek the stage lost in him! Lovegrove, who came nearest to the old actors, revived the character some few seasons ago, and made it sufficiently grotesque; but Dodd was *it*, as it came out of Nature's hands. It might be said to remain *in puris naturalibus*. In expressing slowness of apprehension, this actor sur- passed all others. You could see the first dawn of an idea stealing slowly over his countenance, climb- ing up by little and little, with a painful process, till it cleared up at last to the fulness of a twilight conception—its highest meridian. He seemed to keep back his intellect, as some have had the power to retard their pulsation. The balloon takes less time in filling than it took to cover the expansion of his broad moony face over all its quarters with

expression. A glimmer of understanding would
appear in a corner of his eye, and for lack of fuel go
out again. A part of his forehead would catch a
little intelligence, and be a long time in communi-
cating it to the remainder.

I am ill at dates, but I think it is now better than
five-and-twenty years ago, that walking in the
gardens of Gray's Inn,—they were then far finer
than they are now; the accursed Verulam Buildings
had not encroached upon all the east side of them,
cutting out delicate green crankles, and shouldering
away one of two of the stately alcoves of the
terrace—the survivor stands gaping and relationless
as if it remembered its brother—they are still the
best gardens of any of the Inns of Court, my
beloved Temple not forgotten—have the gravest
character; their aspect being altogether reverend
and law-breathing; Bacon has left the impress of
his foot upon their gravel walks; taking my afternoon solace on a summer day upon the aforesaid
terrace, a comely, sad personage came towards me,
whom, from his grave air and deportment, I judged
to be one of the old Benchers of the Inn. He had
a serious, thoughtful forehead, and seemed to be in
meditations of mortality. As I have an instinctive
awe of old Benchers, I was passing him with that
sort of sub-indicative token of respect which one is
apt to demonstrate towards a venerable stranger,
and which rather denotes an inclination to greet
him, than any positive motion of the body to that
effect, (a species of humility and will-worship which

I observe, nine times out of ten, rather puzzles than
pleases the person it is offered to), when the face,
turning full upon me, strangely identified itself
with that of Dodd. Upon close inspection I was
not mistaken. But could this sad thoughtful
countenance be the same vacant face of folly which
I had hailed so often under circumstances of gaiety;
which I had never seen without a smile, or recognised but as the usher of mirth ; that looked out so
formally flat in Foppington, so frothily pert in
Tattle, so impotently busy in Backbite; so blankly
divested of all meaning, or resolutely expressive
of none, in Acres, in Fribble, and a thousand
agreeable impertinences ? Was this the face,
full of thought and carefulness, that had so often
divested itself at will of every trace of either to
give me diversion, to clear my cloudy face for
two or three hours at least of its furrows ? Was
this the face—manly, sober, intelligent—which I
had so often despised, made mocks at, made merry
with ? The remembrance of the freedoms which I
had taken with it came upon me with a reproach of
insult. I could have asked it pardon. I thought
it looked upon me with a sense of injury. There
is something strange as well as sad in seeing actors,
your pleasant fellows particularly, subjected to and
suffering the common lot ; their fortunes, their
casualties, their deaths, seem to belong to the scene,
their actions to be amenable to poetic justice only.
We can hardly connect them with more awful responsibilities. The death of this fine actor took

place shortly after this meeting. He had quitted the stage some months; and, as I learned afterwards, had been in the habit of resorting daily to these gardens, almost to the day of his decease. In these serious walks, probably, he was divesting himself of many scenic and some real vanities, weaning himself from the frivolities of the lesser and the greater theatre—doing gentle penance for a life of no very reprehensible fooleries — taking off by degrees the buffoon mask, which he might feel he had worn too long—and rehearsing for a more solemn cast of part. Dying, he ' put on the weeds of Dominic.'*

If few can remember Dodd, many yet living will not easily forget the pleasant creature who in those days enacted the part of the Clown to Dodd's Sir Andrew. Richard, or rather Dicky Suett—for so in his life-time he delighted to be called, and time hath ratified the appellation—lieth buried on the north side of the cemetery of Holy Paul, to whose service his nonage and tender years were dedicated. There are who do yet remember him at that period —his pipe clear and harmonious. He would often

---

* Dodd was a man of reading, and left at his death a choice collection of old English literature. I should judge him to have been a man of wit. I know one instance of an impromptu which no length of study could have bettered. My merry friend, Jem White had seen Dodd one evening in Aguecheek, and recognising him the next day in Fleet Street, was irresistibly impelled to take off his hat and salute him as the identical Knight of the preceding evening with a ' Save you, *Sir Andrew.*' Dodd, not at all disconcerted at this unusual address from a stranger, with a courteous half-rebuking wave of the hand, put him off with an ' Away, *Fool!*'

speak of his chorister days, when he was 'cherub Dicky.'

What clipped his wings, or made it expedient that he should exchange the holy for the profane state; whether he had lost his good voice, (his best recommendation to that office), like Sir John, 'with hallooing and singing of anthems;' or whether he was adjudged to lack something, even in those early years, of the gravity indispensable to an occupation which professeth to 'commerce with the skies,'—I could never rightly learn; but we find him, after the probation of a twelvemonth or so, reverting to a secular condition, and become one of us.

I think he was not altogether of that timber out of which cathedral seats and sounding-boards are hewed. But if a glad heart,—kind, and therefore glad—be any part of sanctity, then might the robe of Motley, with which he invested himself with so much humility after his deprivation, and which he wore so long with so much blameless satisfaction to himself and to the public, be accepted for a surplice—his white stole, and *albe*.

The first fruits of his secularisation was an engagement upon the boards of Old Drury, at which theatre he commenced, as I have been told, with adopting the manner of Parsons in old men's characters. At the period in which most of us knew him, he was no more an imitator than he was in any true sense himself imitable.

He was the Robin Goodfellow of the stage. He

E

came in to trouble all things with a welcome perplexity, himself no whit troubled for the matter.
He was known, like Puck, by his note—*Ha! Ha!
Ha!*—sometimes deepening to *Ho! Ho! Ho!* with
an irresistible accession, derived, perhaps, remotely
from his ecclesiastical education, foreign to his
prototype of—*O La!* Thousands of hearts yet
respond to the chuckling *O La!* of Dickey Suett,
brought back to their remembrance by the faithful
transcript of his friend Matthew's mimicry. The
'force of nature could no further go.' He drolled
upon the stock of these two syllables richer than
the cuckoo.

Care, that troubles all the world, was forgotten
in his composition. Had he had but two grains
(nay, half a grain) of it, he could never have supported himself upon those two spider's strings,
which served him (in the latter part of his unmixed
existence) as legs. A doubt or a scruple must
have made him totter, a sigh have puffed him
down; the weight of a frown had staggered him,
a wrinkle made him lose his balance. But on he
went, scrambling upon those airy stilts of his, with
Robin Goodfellow, 'through brake, through briar,
reckless of a scratched face or a torn doublet.'

Shakspeare foresaw him, when he framed his
fools and jesters. They have all the true Suett
stamp, a loose and shambling gait, a slippery
tongue, this last the ready midwife to a without-
pain-delivered jest; in words, light as air, venting
truths deep as the centre; with idlest rhymes

tagging conceit when busiest, singing with Lear in
the tempest, or Sir Toby at the buttery-hatch.

Jack Bannister and he had the fortune to be
more of personal favourites with the town than
any actors before or after. The difference, I take
it, was this:—Jack was more *beloved* for his sweet,
good-natured, moral pretensions. Dicky was more
liked for his sweet, good-natured, no pretensions at
all. Your whole conscience stirred with Bannister's
performance of Walter in the *Children in the Wood*;
but Dicky seemed like a thing, as Shakspeare says
of love, too young to know what conscience is. He
put us into Vesta's days. Evil fled before him—
not as from Jack, as from an antagonist—but
because it could not touch him, any more than a
cannon ball a fly. He was delivered from the
burthen of that death; and, when death came himself, not in a metaphor, to fetch Dicky, it is
recorded of him by Robert Palmer, who kindly
watched his exit, that he received the last stroke,
neither varying his accustomed tranquillity, nor
tune, with the simple exclamation, worthy to have
been recorded in his epitaph—*O La! O La! Bobby!*

The elder Palmer (of stage treading celebrity)
commonly played Sir Toby in those days; but
there is a solidity of wit in the jests of that half-
Falstaff which he did not quite fill out. He was as
much too showy as Moody (who sometimes took
the part) was dry and sottish. In sock or buskin
there was an air of swaggering gentility about
Jack Palmer. He was a *gentleman* with a slight

infusion of *the footman*. His brother Bob, (of recenter memory,) who was his shadow in every-thing while he lived, and dwindled into less than a shadow afterwards, was a *gentleman* with a little stronger infusion of the *latter ingredient*; that was all. It is amazing how a little of the more or less makes a difference in these things. When you saw Bobby in the Duke's Servant,* you said 'What a pity such a pretty fellow was only a servant!' When you saw Jack figuring in Captain Absolute, you thought you could trace his promotion to some lady of quality who fancied the handsome fellow in topknot, and had bought him a commission. There-fore Jack in Dick Amlet was insuperable.

Jack had two voices, both plausible, hypocritical, and insinuating; but his secondary or supplemental voice still more decisively histrionic than his com-mon one. It was reserved for the spectator; and the *dramatis personœ* were supposed to know nothing at all about it. The *lies* of Young Wilding, and the *sentiments* in Joseph Surface, were thus marked out in a sort of italics to the audience. This secret correspondence with the company before the curtain (which is the bane and death of tragedy) has an extremely happy effect in some kinds of comedy, in the more highly artificial comedy of Congreve, or of Sheridan especially, where the absolute sense of reality (so indispensible to scenes of interest) is not required, or would rather inter-

---

* 'High Life Below Stairs.'

fere to diminish your pleasure. The fact is, you do not believe in such characters as Surface—the villain of artificial comedy—even while you read or see them. If you did, they would shock and not divert you. When Ben, in *Love for Love*, returns from sea, the following exquisite dialogue occurs at his first meeting with his father:—

Sir Sampson. Thou hast been many a weary league, Ben, since I saw thee.

Ben. Ey, ey, been? Been far enough, and that be all. Well, father, and how do all at home? How does brother Dick, and brother Val?

Sir Sampson. Dick! body o' me, Dick has been dead these two years. I writ you word when you were at Leghorn.

Ben. Mess, that's true: Marry, I had forgot. Dick is dead, as you say. Well, and how, I have a many questions to ask you.

Here is an instance of insensibility which in real life would be revolting, or rather in real life could not have co-existed with the warm-hearted temperament of the character. But when you read it in the spirit with which such playful selections and specious combinations rather than strict *metaphrases* of nature should be taken, or when you saw Bannister play it, it neither did, nor does, wound the moral sense at all. For what is Ben — the pleasant sailor which Bannister gives us—but a piece of satire—a creation of Congreve's fancy—a dreamy combination of all the accidents of a sailor's character—his contempt of money—his credulity to women—with that necessary estrangement from home which it is just within the verge of credibility to suppose *might* produce such an hallucination as is here described. We never think the worse of

Ben for it, or feel it as a stain upon his character.
But when an actor comes, and instead of the delightful phantom—the creature dear to half-belief,
which Bannister exhibited — displays before our
eyes a downright concretion of a Wapping sailor, a
jolly, warm-hearted Jack Tar, and nothing else;
while instead of investing it with a delicious confusedness of the head, and a veering undirected
goodness of purpose, he gives to it a downright daylight understanding, and a full consciousness of its
actions; thrusting forward the sensibilities of the
character with a pretence as if it stood upon nothing
else, and was to be judged by them alone—we feel
the discord of the thing; the scene is disturbed; a
real man has got in among the *dramatis personæ,*
and puts them out.   We want the sailor turned out.
We feel that his true place is not behind the curtain.
but in the first or second gallery.

THE artificial Comedy, or Comedy of manners, is quite extinct on our stage. Congreve and Farquhar show their heads once in seven years only, to be exploded and put down instantly. The times cannot bear them. Is it for a few wild speeches, an occasional licence of dialogue? I think not altogether. The business of their dramatic characters will not stand the moral test. We screw everything up to that. Idle gallantry in a fiction, a dream, the passing pageant of an evening, startles us in the same way as the alarming indications of profligacy in a son or ward in real life should startle a parent or guardian. We have no such middle emotions as dramatic in-terests left. We see a stage libertine playing his

loose pranks of two hours' duration, and of no after
consequence, with the severe eyes which inspect real
vices with their bearings upon two worlds. We are
spectators to a plot or intrigue, (not reducible in life
to the point of strict morality), and take it all for
truth. We substitute a real for a dramatic person,
and judge him accordingly. We try him in our
courts, from which there is no appeal to the *dramatis
personæ*, his peers. We have been spoiled with—not
sentimental comedy—but a tyrant far more pernicious to our pleasures which has succeeded to it,
the exclusive and all-devouring drama of common
life; where the moral point is everything; where,
instead of the fictitious half-believed personages of
the stage, (the phantoms of old comedy), we recognise ourselves, our brothers, aunts, kinsfolk, allies,
patrons, enemies,—the same as in life,—with an interest in what is going on so hearty and substantial,
that we cannot afford our moral judgment, in its
deepest and most vital results, to compromise or
slumber for a moment. What is *there* transacting,
by no modification is made to affect us in any other
manner than the same events or characters would
do in our relationships of life. We carry our fireside concerns to the theatre with us. We do not
go thither like our ancestors, to escape from the
pressure of reality, so much as to confirm our experience of it; to make assurance double, and take
a bond of fate. We must live our toilsome lives
twice over, as it was the mournful privilege of
Ulysses to descend twice to the shades. All that

neutral ground of character, which stood between vice and virtue; or which in fact was indifferent to neither, where neither properly was called in question; that happy breathing-place from the burthen of a perpetual moral questioning—the sanctuary and quiet Alsatia of hunted causistry— is broken up and disfranchised, and injurious to the interests of society. The privileges of the place are taken away by law. We dare not dally with images, or names, of wrong. We bark like foolish dogs at shadows. We dread infection from the scenic representation of disorder, and fear a painted pustule. In our anxiety that our morality should not take cold, we wrap it up in a great blanket sur- tout of precaution against the breeze and sunshine.

I confess for myself that (with no great delin- quencies to answer for) I am glad for a season to take an air beyond the diocese of the strict con- science—not to live always in the precincts of the Law Courts—but now and then, for a dream-while or so to imagine a world with no meddling restric- tions—to get into recesses, whither the hunter cannot follow me—

> ————Secret shades
> Of woody Ida's inmost grove,
> While yet there was no fear of Jove.

I come back to my cage and my restraint the fresher and more healthy for it. I wear my shackles more contentedly for having respired the breath of an imaginary freedom. I do not know how it is with others, but I feel the better always for the perusal of one of Congreve's—nay, why should I not add even of Wycherley's—comedies. I am the gayer at least for it; and I could never connect those sports of a witty fancy in any shape with any result to be drawn from them to imitation in real life. They are a world of themselves almost as much as fairy-land. Take one of their characters, male or female (with few exceptions they are alike), and place it in a modern play, and my virtuous indignation shall rise against the profligate wretch as warmly as the Catos of the pit could desire; because in a modern play I am to judge of the right and the wrong. The standard of *police* is the measure of *political justice*. The atmosphere will blight it; it cannot live here. It has got into a moral world, where it has got no business, from which it must needs fall headlong; as dizzy and incapable of making a stand as a Swedenborgian bad spirit that has wandered unawares into the sphere of one of his Good Men or Angels. But in its own world do we feel the creature is so very bad? The Fainalls and the Mirabels, the Dorimants and the Lady Touchwoods, in their own sphere, do not offend my moral sense; in fact they do not appeal to it at all. They seem engaged in their proper element. They break through no laws or conscientious restraints. They know of none. They have got out of Christendom into the land—what shall I call it? of cuckoldry—the Utopia of gallantry, where pleasure is duty, and the manners perfect freedom. It is altogether a speculative scene of things, which has no reference whatever to the world that is. No good person can be justly offended as a spectator, because no good person suffers on the stage. Judged morally every character in these plays—the few exceptions only are *mistakes*— is alike essentially vain and worthless. The great art of Congreve is especially shown in this, that he has entirely excluded from his scenes (some little generosities in the part of Angelica perhaps excepted) not only anything like a faultless character, but any pretensions to goodness or good feelings whatsoever. Whether he did this designedly, or instinctively, the effect is as happy as the design (if design) was bold. I used to wonder at the strange power which his 'Way of the World' in particular possesses of interesting you all along in the pursuit of characters, for whom you absolutely care nothing—for you neither hate nor love his personages—and I think it is owing to this very indifference for any that you endure the whole. He has spread a privation of moral light, I will call it, rather than by the ugly name of palpable darkness, over his creations; and his shadows flit before you without distinction or preference. Had he introduced a good character, a single gush of moral feeling, a revulsion of the judgment to actual life and actual duties, the impertinent Goschen would only have lighted to the discovery of deformities, which are now none, because we think them none.

Translated into real life, the characters of his and his friend Wycherley's dramas are profligates and strumpets,—the business of their brief existence, the undivided pursuit of lawless gallantry. No other spring of action, or possible motive of conduct, is recognised; principles which, universally acted upon, must reduce this frame of things to a chaos. But we do them wrong in so translating them. No such effects are produced, in *their* world. When we are among them, we are amongst a chaotic people. We are not to judge them by our usages. No reverend institutions are insulted by their proceedings, for they have none among them. No peace of families is violated, for no family ties exist among them. No purity of the marriage bed is stained, for none is supposed to have a being. No deep affections are disquieted, no holy wedlock bands are snapped asunder, for affection's depth and wedded faith are not of the growth of that soil. There is neither right nor wrong, gratitude or its opposite, claim or duty, paternity or sonship. Of what consequence is it to Virtue, or how is she at all concerned about it, whether Sir Simon or Dapperwit steals away Miss Martha; or who is the father of Lord Froth's or Sir Paul Pliant's children ?

The whole is a passing pageant, where we should sit as unconcerned at the issues, for life or death, as at a battle of the frogs and mice. But, like Don Quixote, we take part against the puppets, and quite as impertinently. We dare not contemplate an Atlantis, a scheme out of which our coxcombical moral sense is for a little transitory ease excluded. We have not the courage to imagine a state of things for which there is neither reward nor punishment. We cling to the painful necessities of shame and blame. We would indict our very dreams.

Amidst the mortifying circumstances attendant upon growing old, it is something to have seen the *School for Scandal* in its glory. This comedy grew out of Congreve and Wycherley, but gathered some allays of the sentimental comedy which follow theirs. It is impossible that it should be now *acted*, though it continues, at long intervals, to be announced in the bills. Its hero, when Palmer played it at least, was Joseph Surface. When I remember the gay boldness, the graceful solemn plausibility, the measured step, the insinuating voice, (to express it in a word), the downright *acted* villany of the part, so different from the pressure of conscious actual wickedness, the hypocritical assumption of hypocrisy, which made Jack so deservedly a favourite in that character, I must needs conclude the present generation of playgoers more virtuous than myself, or more dense. I freely confess that he divided the palm with me with his better brother; that, in fact, I like him quite as well. Not but there are passages, like that, for instance, where Joseph is made to refuse a pittance to a poor relation—incongruities which Sheridan was forced upon by the attempt to join the artificial with the sentimental comedy, either of which must destroy the

other; but over these obstructions Jack's manner
floated him so lightly, that a refusal from him no
more shocked you, than the easy compliance of
Charles gave you in reality any pleasure; you got
over the paltry question as quickly as you could,
to get back into the regions of pure comedy, where
no cold moral reigns. The highly artificial manner
of Palmer in this character counteracted every disagreeable impression which you might have received
from the contrast, supposing them real, between the
two brothers. You did not believe in Joseph with
the same faith with which you believed in Charles.
The latter was a pleasant reality, the former a no
less pleasant poetical foil to it. The comedy, I have
said, is incongruous; a mixture of Congreve with
sentimental incompatibilities; the gaiety upon the
whole is buoyant; but it required the consummate
art of Palmer to reconcile the discordant elements.

A player with Jack's talents, if we had one now,
would not dare to do the part in the same manner.
He would instinctively avoid every turn which
might tend to unrealise, and so to make the character
fascinating. He must take his cue from the spectators, who would expect a bad man and a good
man as rigidly opposed to each other as the death-
bed of these geniuses are contrasted in the prints,
which I am sorry to say have disappeared from the
windows of my old friend Carrington Bowles, of
St Paul's Churchyard memory—(an exhibition as
venerable as the adjacent cathedral, and almost
coeval) of the bad and good man at the hour of

death; where the ghastly apprehensions of the former, and truly the grim phantom with his reality of a toasting-fork is not to be despised, so finely contrast with the meek complacent kissing of the rod—taking it in like honey and butter—with which the latter submits to the scythe of the gentle bleeder, Time, who wields his lancet with the apprehensive finger of a popular young ladies' surgeon. What flesh like loving grass, would not covet to meet half-way the stroke of such a delicate mower? John Palmer was twice an actor in this exquisite part. He was playing to you all the while that he was playing upon Sir Peter and his lady. You had the first intimation of a sentiment before it was on his lips. His altered voice was meant for you, and you were to suppose that his fictitious co-flutterers on the stage perceived nothing at all of it. What was it to you if that half-reality, the husband, was over-reached by the puppetry, or the thin thing (Lady Teazle's reputation) was persuaded it was dying of a plethory? The fortunes of Othello and Desdemona were not concerned in it. Poor Jack has passed from the stage in good time, that he did not live to this our age of seriousness. The pleasant old Teazle *King*, too, is gone in good time. His manner would scarce have passed current in our day. We must love or hate, acquit or condemn, censure or pity, exert our detestable coxcombry of moral judgment upon every thing. Joseph Surface to go down now, must be a downright revolting villain—no compromise; his first appearance must shock and give horror; his spacious plausibilities, which the pleasurable faculties of our fathers welcomed with such hearty greetings, knowing that no harm (dramatic harm even) could come, or was meant to come of them, must inspire a cold and killing aversion. Charles, the real canting person of the scene, (for the hypocrisy of Joseph has its ulterior legitimate ends, but his brother's professions of a good heart centre in downright self-satisfaction), must be *loved*, and Joseph *hated*. To balance one disagreeable reality with another, Sir Peter Teazle must be no longer the comic idea of a fretful old bachelor bridegroom, whose teasings (while King acted it) were evidently as much played off at you as they were meant to concern anybody on the stage —he must be a real person, capable in law of sustaining an injury—a person towards whom duties are to be acknowledged—the genuine crim. con. antagonist of the villanous seducer Joseph. To realise him more, his sufferings under his unfortunate match must have the downright pungency of life—must (or should) make you not mirthful but uncomfortable, just as the same predicament would move you in a neighbour or old friend. The delicious scenes which give the play its name and zest, must affect you in the same serious manner as if you heard the reputation of a dear female friend, attacked in your real presence. Crabtree and Sir Benjamin—those poor snakes that live but in the sunshine of your mirth—must be ripened by this hot-bed process of realisation into asps or amphis-

bænas; and Mrs Candour (Oh, frightful!) become a
hooded serpent. Oh! who that remembers Parsons
and Dodd—the wasp and butterfly of the School
for Scandal—in those two characters, and charming
natural Miss Pope, the perfect gentlewoman as distinguished from the fine lady of comedy, in this
latter part, would forego the true scenic delight, the
escape from life, the oblivion of consequences, the
holiday barring out of the pedant Reflection, those
Saturnalia of two or three brief hours, well won
from the world, to sit instead at one of our modern
plays, to have his coward conscience (that forsooth
must not be left for a moment) stimulated with
perpetual appeals, dulled rather, and blunted, as a
faculty without repose must be, and his moral
vanity pampered with images of notional justice,
notional beneficence, lives saved without the spectator's risk, and fortunes given away that cost the
author nothing?

No piece was perhaps ever so completely cast in
all its parts as this *manager's comedy.* Miss Farren
had succeeded to Mrs Abington in Lady Teazle;
and Smith, the original Charles, had retired when
I first saw it. The rest of the characters, with
very slight exceptions, remained. I remember it
was then the fashion to cry down John Kemble,
who took the part of Charles after Smith, but
I thought very unjustly. Smith, I fancy, was
more airy, and took the eye with a certain gaiety
of person. He brought with him no sombre re-
collections of tragedy. He had not to expiate the

F

fault of having pleased beforehand in lofty declamation. He had no sins of Hamlet or of
Richard to atone for. His failure in these parts
was a passport to success in one of so opposite
a tendency. But, as far as I could judge, the
weighty sense of Kemble made up for more personal incapacity than he had to answer for. His
harshest tones in this part came steeped and
dulcified in good humour. He made his defects
a grace. His exact declamatory manner, as he
managed it, only served to convey the points
of his dialogue with more precision. It seemed
to head the shafts to carry them deeper. Not
one of his sparkling sentences was lost. I remember minutely how he delivered each in
succession, and cannot by any effort imagine
how any of them could be altered for the better.
No man could deliver brilliant dialogue, the
dialogue of Congreve or of Wycherley, because
none understood it half so well as John Kemble.
His Valentine, in *Love for Love*, was, to my re-
collection, faultless. He flagged sometimes in
the intervals of tragic passion. He would slumber
over the level parts of an heroic character. His
Macbeth had been known to nod. But he always
seemed to me to be particularly alive to pointed
and witty dialogue. The relaxing levities of
tragedy had not been touched by any since him ;
the playful court-bred spirit in which he condescended to the players in Hamlet—the sportive
relief which he threw into the darker shades of

Richard, disappeared with him. He had his
sluggish moods, his torpors, but they were the
halting stones and resting place of his tragedy
—politic savings, and fetches of the breath—
husbandry of the lungs, where Nature pointed
him to be an economist, rather, I think, than errors
of the judgment. They were, at worst, less painful
than the eternal tormenting unappeasable vigilance,
the 'lidless dragon eyes,' of present fashionable
tragedy.

NOT many nights ago I had come home from seeing this extraordinary performer in *Cockletop*; and when I retired to my pillow his whimsical image still stuck by me in a manner as to threaten sleep. In vain I tried to divest myself of it, by conjuring up the most opposite associations. I resolved to be serious. I raised up the gravest topics of life; private misery, public calamity. All would not do:

———There the antic sate
Mocking our state———

his queer visnomy, his bewildering costume, all the strange things which he had raked together, his serpentine rod swagging about in his pocket, Cleo-

patra's tear, and the rest of his relics, O'Keefe's
wild farce, and *his* wilder commentary, till the
passion of laughter, like grief in excess, relieved
itself by its own weight, inviting the sleep which
in the first instance it had driven away.

But I was not to escape so easily. No sooner
did I fall into slumbers, than the same image, only
more perplexing, assailed me in the shape of
dreams. Not one Munden, but five hundred, were
dancing before me, like the faces which, whether
you will or no, come when you have been taking
opium—all the strange combinations, which this
strangest of all strange mortals ever shot his proper
countenance into, from the day he came commissioned to dry up the tears of the town for the loss
of the now almost forgotten Edwin. Oh, for the
power of the pencil to have fixed them when I
awoke! A season or two since, there was exhibited
a Hogarth Gallery. I do not see why there should
not be a Munden Gallery. In richness and variety,
the latter would not fall far short of the former.

'There is one face of Farley, one face of Knight,
one (but what a one it is!) of Liston; but Munden
has none that you can properly pin down and call
his. When you think he has exhausted his battery
of looks, in unaccountable warfare with your gravity, suddenly he sprouts out an entirely new set
of features, like Hydra. He is not one, but legion;
not so much a comedian as a company. If his
name could be multiplied like his countenance, it
might fill a play-bill. He, and he alone, literally

makes faces: applied to any other person, the phrase is a mere figure, denoting certain modifications of the human countenance. Out of some invisible wardrobe he dips for faces, as his friend Suett used for wigs, and fetches them out as easily. I should not be surprised to see him some day put out the head of a river-horse; or come forth a pewitt, or lapwing, some feathered metamorphosis.

I have seen this gifted actor in Sir Christopher Curry, in old Dornton, diffuse a glow of sentiment which has made the pulse of a crowded theatre beat like that of one man, when he has come in aid of the pulpit, doing good to the moral heart of a people. I have seen some faint approaches to this sort of excellence in other players. But in the grand grotesque of farce, Munden stands out as single and unaccompanied as Hogarth. Hogarth, strange to tell, had no followers. The school of Munden began, and must end, with himself.

Can any man *wonder* like he does? can any man *see ghosts* like he does? or *fight with his own shadow,* 'SESSA,' as he does in that strangely-neglected thing, *The Cobbler of Preston,* where his alternations from the Cobbler to the Magnifico, and from the Magnifico to the Cobbler, keep the brain of the spectator in as wild a ferment, as if some Arabian Night were being acted before him? Who like him can throw, or ever attempted to throw, a preternatural interest over the commonest

daily life objects? A table or a joint stool, in
his conception, rises into a dignity equivalent to
Cassiopeia's chair. It is invested with con-
stellatory importance. You could not speak of
it with more deference, if it were mounted into
the firmament. A beggar in the hands of Michael
Angelo, says Fuseli, rose the Patriarch of Poverty.
So the gusto of Munden antiquates and ennobles
what it touches. His pots and his ladles are as
grand and primal as the seething-pots and hooks
seen in old prophetic vision. A tub of butter,
contemplated by him, amounts to a Platonic idea.
He understands a leg of mutton in its quiddity.
He stands wondering, amid the common - place
materials of life, like primæval man with the sun
and stars about him.

'DEAR SIR,—Your communication to me of the death of Munden made me weep. Now, sir, I am not of the melting mood; but in these serious times, the loss of half the world's fun is no trivial deprivation. It was my loss (or *gain* shall I call it ?) in the early time of my play-going, to have missed all Munden's acting. There were only he and Lewis at Covent Garden, while Drury Lane was exuberant with Parsons, Dodd, &c., such a comic company as, I suppose, the stage never showed. Thence, in the evening of my life, I had Munden all to myself, more mellowed, richer, perhaps, than ever. I cannot say what his change of faces produced in me. It was not acting. He was not one of my 'old actors.' It might be better.

His power was extravagant. I saw him one even-
ing in three drunken characters. Three farces
were played. One part was Dozey—I forget the
rest—but they were so discriminated, that a
stranger might have seen them all, and not have
dreamed that he was seeing the same actor. I am
jealous for the actors who pleased my youth. He
was not a Parsons or a Dodd, but he was more
wonderful. He seemed as if he could *do* anything.
He was not an actor, but something *better*, if you
please. Shall I instance Old Foresight in *Love for
Love*, in which Parsons was at once the old man,
the astrologer, &c. Munden dropped the old man,
the doater—which makes the character—but he
substituted for it a moon-struck character, a perfect abstraction from this earth, that looked as if
he had newly come down from the planets. Now,
that is not what I call *acting*. It might be better.
He was imaginative; he could impress upon an
audience an *idea*—the low one perhaps of a leg of
mutton and turnips; but such was the grandeur
and singleness of his expressions, that that single
expression would convey to all his auditory a
notion of all the pleasures they had all received
from all the legs of mutton *and turnips* they had
ever eaten in their lives. Now, this is not *acting*
Nor do I set down Munden amongst my old actors
He was only a wonderful man, exerting his vivid
impressions through the agency of the stage. In
one only thing did I see him *act*—that is, support
a character, it was in a wretched farce called

Johnny Gilpin, for Dowton's benefit, in which he did a Cockney; the thing run but one night; but when I say that Liston's Lubin's Log was nothing to it, I say little; it was transcendent. And here, let me say of actors—*envious* actors—that of *Munden,* Liston was used to speak, almost with the enthusiasm due to the dead, in terms of such allowed superiority to every actor on the stage, and this at a time when Munden was gone by in the world's estimation, that it convinced me that *artists* (in which term I include poets, painters, &c.) are not so envious as the world think. I have little time, and therefore enclose a criticism on Munden's Old Dozey and his general acting, by a gentleman, who attends less to these things than formerly, but whose criticism I think masterly.

'C. LAMB.'

'Mr Munden appears to us to be the most *classical* of actors. He is that in high farce which Kemble was in high tragedy. The lines of these great artists are, it must be admitted, sufficiently distinct; but the same elements are in both,—the same directness of purpose, the same singleness of aim, the same concentration of power, the same iron-casing of inflexible manner, the same statue-like precision of gesture, movement, and attitude. The hero of farce is as little affected with impulses from without, as the retired Prince of Tragedians. There is something solid, sterling, almost adamantine, in the building up of his most grotesque characters. When he fixes his wonder-working face in any of its most amazing varieties, it looks as if the picture were carved out from a rock by Nature in a sportive vein, and might last for ever. It is like what we can imagine a mask of the old Grecian Comedy to have been, only that it lives, and breathes, and changes. His most fantastical gestures are the grand ideal of farce. He seems as though he belonged to the earliest and the stateliest age of Comedy, when instead of superficial foibles and the airy varieties of fashion, she had the grand asperities of man to work on, when her grotesque images had something romantic about them, and when humour and parody were themselves heroic. His expressions of feeling and bursts of enthusiasm are among the most genuine which we have ever felt. They seem to come up from a depth of emotion in the heart, and burst through the sturdy casing of manner with a strength which seems increased tenfold by its real and hearty obstacle. The workings of his spirit seem to expand his frame, till we can scarcely believe that by measure it is small : for the space which he fills in the imagination is so real, that we almost mistake it for that of corporeal dimensions. His *Old Dozey*, in the excellent farce of ' Past Ten o'Clock,' is his grandest effort of this kind, and we know of nothing finer. He seems to have a ' heart of oak ' indeed. His description of a sea-fight is the most noble and triumphant piece of enthusiasm which we remember. It is as if the spirits of a whole crew of nameless heroes " were swelling in his bosom." We never felt so ardent and proud a sympathy with the valour of England as when we heard it. May health long be his, thus to do our hearts good ; for we never saw any actor whose merits have the least resemblance to his, even in species ; and when his genius is withdrawn from the stage, we shall not have left even a term by which we can fitly describe it.'

My acquaintance with the pleasant creature, whose loss we all deplore, was but slight.

My first introduction to Elliston, which afterwards ripened into an acquaintance a little on this side of intimacy, was over a counter in the Leamington Spa Library, then newly entered upon by a branch of his family. Elliston, whom nothing misbecame—to auspicate, I suppose, the filial concern, and set it a-going with a lustre—was serving in person, two damsels fair, who had come into the shop ostensibly to inquire for some new publication, but in reality to have a sight at the illustrious shopman, hoping some conference. With what an air did he reach down the volume, dispassionately giving his opinion of the work in question, and

launching out into a dissertation on its comparative
merits with those of certain publications of a similar
stamp, its rivals; his enchanted customers fairly
hanging on his lips, subdued to their authoritative
sentence. So I have seen a gentleman in comedy
acting the shopman. So Lovelace sold his gloves
in King Street. I admired the histrionic art by
which he contrived to carry clean away every
notion of disgrace, from the occupation he had so
generously submitted to; and from that hour I
judged him, with no after repentance, to be a person
with whom it would be a felicity to be more acquainted.

To descant upon his merits as a Comedian would
be superfluous. With this blended private and professional habits alone I have to do; that harmonious
fusion of the manners of the player into those of
every-day life, which brought the stage boards into
streets and dining-parlours, and kept up the play
when the play was ended. 'I like Wrench,' a friend
was saying to him one day, 'because he is the same
natural, easy creature *on* the stage that he is *off.*'
'My case exactly,' retorted Elliston, with a charming forgetfulness that the converse of a proposition
does not always lead to the same conclusion, 'I
am the same person *off* the stage that I am *on.*'
The inference, at first sight, seems identical; but
examine it a little, and it confesses only that the
one performer was never, and the other always,
acting.

And in truth this was the charm of Elliston's

private deportment. You had spirited performance always going on before your eyes, with nothing to pay. As where a monarch takes up his casual abode for a night, the poorest hovel which he honours by his sleeping in it, becomes *ipso facto* for that time a palace; so wherever Elliston walked, sate, or stood still, there was the theatre He carried about with him his pit, boxes, and galleries, and set up his portable playhouse at corners of streets, and in the market-places. Upon flintiest pavements he trod the boards still; and if his theme chanced to be passionate, the green baize carpet of tragedy spontaneously rose beneath his feet. Now, this was hearty, and showed a love for his art. So Apelles *always* painted, in thought. So G. D. *always* poetises. I hate a lukewarm artist. I have known actors, and some of them of Elliston's own stamp, who shall have agreeably been amusing you in the part of a rake or a coxcomb, through the two or three hours of their dramatic existence; but no sooner does the curtain fall with its leaden clatter, but a spirit of lead seems to seize on all their faculties. They emerge sour, morose persons, intolerable to their families, servants, &c. Another shall have been expanding your heart with generous deeds and sentiments, till it even beats with yearnings of universal sympathy; you absolutely long to go home and do some good action. The play seems tedious till you can get fairly out of the house, and realize your laudable intentions. At length the final bell rings, and this cordial representative of

all that is amiable in human breasts steps forth a
miser. Elliston was more of a piece. Did he *play*
Ranger? and did Ranger fill the general bosom of
the town with satisfaction? why should *he* not be
Ranger, and diffuse the same cordial satisfaction
among his private circles? With *his* temperament,
his animal spirits, *his* good-nature, *his* follies perchance, could he do better than identify himself
with his impersonation? Are we to like a pleasant
rake or coxcomb on the stage, and give ourselves
airs of aversion for the identical character, presented to us in actual life? or what would the performer have gained by divesting himself of the
impersonation? Could the man Elliston have been
essentially different from his part, even if he had
avoided to reflect to us studiously, in private circles,
and airy briskness, the forwardness, and scape-
goat trickeries of his prototype?

'But there is something not natural in this ever-
lasting *acting*; we want the real man.'

Are you quite sure that it is not the man himself, whom you cannot, or will not see, under some
adventitious trappings, which, nevertheless, sit not
at all inconsistently upon him? What, if it is the
nature of some men to be highly artificial? The
fault is least reprehensible in *players*. Cibber was
his own Foppington, with almost as much wit as
Vanbrugh could add to it.

'My conceit of his person' (it is Ben Jonson
speaking of Lord Bacon) 'was never increased towards him by his *place* or *honours;* but I have

and do reverence him for the *greatness* that was
only proper to himself; in that he seemed to me
ever one of the *greatest* men that had been in many
ages. In his adversity I ever prayed that Heaven
would give him strength; for *greatness* he could
not want.'

The quality here commended was scarcely less
conspicuous in the subject of these idle reminis-
cences than in my Lord Verulam. Those who
have imagined that an unexpected elevation to
the direction of a great London Theatre affected the
consequence of Elliston, or at all changed his
nature, knew not the essential *greatness* of the man
whom they disparage. It was my fortune to
encounter him near St Dunstan's Church (which,
with its punctual giants, is now no more than dust
and a shadow), on the morning of his election to
that high office. Grasping my hand with a look of
significance, he only uttered,—' Have you heard
the news?'—then, with another look following up
the blow, he subjoined, ' I am the future manager
of Drury Lane Theatre.'—Breathless as he saw me,
he stayed not for congratulation or reply, but
mutely stalked away, leaving me to chew upon his
new-blown dignities at leisure. In fact, nothing
could be said to it. Expressive silence alone
could muse his praise. This was in his *great* style.

But was he less *great* (be witness, O ye powers
of Equanimity, that supported in the ruins of
Carthage the consular exile, and more recently
transmuted, for a more illustrious exile, the barren

constableship of Elba into an image of Imperial
France), when, in melancholy after-years, again,
much nearer the same spot, I met him, when that
sceptre had been wrested from his hand, and his
dominion was curtailed to the petty managership,
and part proprietorship, of the small Olympic, *his
Elba?* He still played nightly upon the boards of
Drury, but in parts, alas! allotted to him, not magnificently distributed by him. Waiving his great
loss as nothing, and magnificently sinking the sense
of fallen *material* grandeur in the more liberal resentment of depreciations done to his more lofty
intellectual pretensions, 'Have you heard?' (his
customary exordium)—'have you heard,' said he,
'how they treat me? they put me in *comedy.*'
Thought I—but his finger on his lips forbade any
verbal interruption—'where could they have put
you better?' Then, after a pause,—'Where I
formerly played Romeo, I now play Mercutio,'—
and so again he stalked away, neither staying, nor
caring for, responses.

O, it was a rich scene,—but Sir A—— C——,
the best of story-tellers and surgeons, who mends a
lame narrative almost as well as he sets a fracture,
alone could do justice to it,—that I was a witness
to, in the tarnished room (that had once been green)
of that same little Olympic. There, after his depo-
sition from Imperial Drury, he substituted a
throne. That Olympic Hill was his 'highest
heaven;' himself 'Jove in his chair.' There he sat
in state, while before him, on complaint of

prompter, was brought for judgment—how shall I describe her?—one of those little tawdry things that flirt at the tails of choruses—a probationer for the town, in either of its senses—the pertest little drab—a dirty fringe and appendage of the lamp's smoke—who, it seems, on some disapprobation expressed by a 'highly respectable' audience —had precipitately quitted her station on the boards, and withdrawn her small talents in disgust.

'And how dare you,' said her manager,—assuming a censorial severity, which would have crushed the confidence of a Vestris, and disarmed that beautiful rebel herself of her professional caprices, —I verily believe he thought *her* standing before him—'how dare you, madam, withdraw yourself, without a notice, from your theatrical duties?' 'I was hissed, sir.' 'And have you the presumption to decide upon the taste of the town?' 'I don't know that, sir, but I will never stand to be hissed,' was the subjoinder of young Confidence—when, gathering up his features into one significant mass of wonder, pity, and expostulatory indignation, in a lesson never to have been lost upon a creature less forward than she who stood before him, his words were these,—'They have hissed *me*.'

'Twas the identical argument *à fortiori*, which the son of Peleus uses to Lycaon trembling under his lance, to persuade him to take his destiny with a good grace. 'I too am mortal.' And it is to be believed that in both cases the rhetoric missed of its application for want of a proper understanding with the faculties of the respective recipients.

' Quite an Opera pit,' he said to me, as he was courteously conducting me over the benches of his Surrey Theatre, the last retreat and recess of his every-day waning grandeur.

Those who knew Elliston will know the *manner* in which he pronounced the latter sentence of the few words I am about to record. One proud day to me he took his roast mutton with us in the Temple, to which I had superadded a preliminary haddock. After a rather plentiful partaking of the meagre banquet, not unrefreshed with the humbler sort of liquors, I made a sort of apology for the humility of the fare, observing that for my own part I never ate but one dish at dinner. ' I, too, never eat but one thing at dinner,' was his reply ; then after a pause—' reckoning fish as nothing.' The manner was all. It was as if by one peremptory sentence he had decreed the annihilation of all the savoury esculents, which the pleasant and nutritious food-giving Ocean pours forth upon poor humans from her watery bosom. This was *greatness*, tempered with considerate *tenderness* to the feelings of his scanty but welcoming entertainer.

Great wert thou in thy life, Robert William Elliston ! and *not lessened* in thy death, if report speak truly, which says that thou didst direct that thy mortal remains should repose under no inscription but one of pure *Latinity*. Classical was thy bringing up ; and beautiful was the feeling on thy last bed, which, connecting the man with the boy, took thee back to thy latest exercise of imagination, to the days when, undreaming of Theatres and Managerships, thou wert a scholar and an early ripe one, under the roofs builded by the munificent and pious Colet. For thee the Pauline Muses weep. In elegies, that shall silence this crude prose, they shall celebrate thy praise.

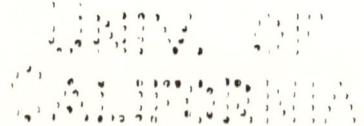

CHARACTERS OF DRAMATIC WRITERS CON-
TEMPORARY WITH SHAKSPEARE

WHEN I selected for publication, in 1808, specimens
of English Dramatic Poets who lived about the time
of Shakspeare, the kind of extracts which I was
anxious to give were, not so much passages of wit
and humour, though the old plays are rich in such,
as scenes of passion, sometimes of the deepest
quality, interesting situations, serious descriptions,
that which is more nearly allied to poetry than to
wit, and to tragic rather than to comic poetry. The
plays which I made choice of were, with few exceptions, such as treat of human life and manners,
rather than masques and Arcadian pastorals, with
their train of abstractions, unimpassioned deities,
passionate mortals—Claius, and Medorus, and

Amintas, and Amaryllis. My leading design was, to illustrate what may be called the moral sense of our ancestors. To show in what manner they felt, when they placed themselves by the power of imagination in trying circumstances, in the conflicts of duty and passion, or the strife of contending duties; what sort of loves and enmities theirs were; how their griefs were tempered, and their full-swoln joys abated; how much of Shakspeare shines in the great men, his contemporaries, and how far in his divine mind and manners he surpassed them and all mankind. I was also desirous to bring together some of the most admired scenes of Fletcher and Massinger, in the estimation of the world the only dramatic poets of that age entitled to be considered after Shakspeare, and, by exhibiting them in the same volume with the more impressive scenes of old Marlowe, Heywood, Tourneur, Webster, Ford, and others, to show what he had slighted, while beyond all proportion we had been crying up one or two favourite names. From the desultory criticisms which accompanied that publication, I have selected a few which I thought would best stand by themselves, as requiring least immediate reference to the play or passage by which they were suggested.

CHRISTOPHER MARLOWE

Lust's Dominion or the Lascivious Queen.— This tragedy is in King Cambyses' vein; rape, and murder, and superlatives; ' huffing braggart puft

lines,' such as the play writers anterior to Shakspeare are full of, and Pistol but coldly imitates.

*Tamburlaine the Great, or the Scythian Shep-
herd.*—The lunes of Tamburlaine are perfect
mid-summer madness. Nebuchadnazar's are mere
modest pretensions compared with the thundering
vaunts of this Scythian Shepherd. He comes in
drawn by conquered kings, and reproaches these
pampered jades of Asia that they can draw but
twenty miles a day. Till I saw this passage with
my own eyes, I never believed that it was anything
more than a pleasant burlesque of mine ancients.
But I can assure my readers that it is soberly set
down in a play, which their ancestors took to be
serious.

Edward the Second.—In a very different style
from mighty Tamburlaine is the tragedy of Edward
the Second. The reluctant pangs of abdicating
royalty in Edward furnished hints, which Shakspeare scarcely improved in his Richard the Second,
and the death scene of Marlowe's King moves pity
and terror beyond any scene ancient or modern
with which I am acquainted.

The Rich Jew of Malta.—Marlowe's Jew does
not approach so near to Shakspeare's, as his Edward
the Second does to Richard the Second. Barabas
is a mere monster, brought in with a large painted
nose to please the rabble. He kills in sport, poisons
whole nunneries, invents infernal machines. He is
just such an exhibition as a century or two earlier
might have been played before the Londoners ' by

the royal command,' when a general pillage and massacre of the Hebrews had been previously resolved on in the Cabinet. It is curious to see a superstition wearing out. The idea of a Jew, which our pious ancestors contemplated with so much horror, has nothing in it now revolting. We have tamed the claws of the beast, and pared its nails, and now we take it to our arms, we fondle it, write plays to flatter it; it is visited by princes, affects a taste, patronises the arts, and is the only liberal and gentleman-like thing in Christendom.

Doctor Faustus.—The growing horrors of Faustus' last scene are awfully marked by the hours and half-hours as they expire, and bring him nearer and nearer to the exactment of his dire compact. It is indeed an agony and a fearful colluctation. Marlowe is said to have been tainted with atheistical positions, to have denied God and the Trinity. To such a genius the history of Faustus must have been delectable food: to wander in fields, where curiosity is forbidden to go, to approach the dark gulf near enough to look in, to be busied in speculations which are the rottenest part of the core of the fruit that fell from the tree of knowledge, *Barabas the Jew, and Faustus the conjurer, are offsprings of a mind which at least delighted to dally with interdicted subjects. They both talk a language which a believer would have been tender

---

* Error, entering into the world with Sin among us poor Adamites, may be said to spring from the tree of knowledge itself, and from the rotten kernels of that fatal apple.—*Howell's Letters.*

of putting into the mouth of a character though but in fiction. But the holiest minds have sometimes not thought it reprehensible to counterfeit impiety in the person of another, to bring Vice upon the stage speaking her own dialect; and, themselves being armed with an unction of self-confident impunity, have not scrupled to handle and touch that familiarly, which would be death to others. Milton in the person of Satan has started speculations hardier than any which the feeble armoury of the atheist ever furnished; and the precise, strait-laced Richardson has strengthened Vice, from the mouth of Lovelace, with entangling sophistries and abstruse pleas against her adversary Virtue, which Sedley, Tilliers, and Rochester, wanted depth of libertinism enough to have invented.

THOMAS DECKER

Old Fortunatus.—The humour of a frantic lover, in the scene where Orleans, to his friend Galloway, defends the passion with which himself, being a prisoner in the English king's court, is enamoured to frenzy of the king's daughter Agripyna, is done to the life. Orleans is as passionate an inamorato as any which Shakspeare ever drew. He is just such another adept in Love's reasons. The sober people of the world are with him—

————————A swarm of fools
Crowding together to be counted wise.

He talks 'pure Biron and Romeo,' he is almost as poetical as they, quite as philosophical, only a little madder. After all, Love's sectaries are a reason unto themselves. We have gone retrograde to the noble heresy, since the days when Sydney proselyted our nation to this mixed health and disease; the kindliest symptom, yet the most alarming crisis in the ticklish state of youth; the nourisher and the destroyer of hopeful wits; the mother of twin births, wisdom and folly, valour and weakness; the servitude above freedom; the gentle mind's religion; the liberal superstition.

The Honest Whore.—There is in the second part of this play, where Bellafront, a reclaimed harlot, recounts some of the miseries of her profession, a simple picture of honour and shame, contrasted without violence, and expressed without immodesty which is worth all the *strong lines* against the harlot's profession, with which both parts of this play are offensively crowded. A satirist is always to be suspected, who, to make vice odious, dwells upon all its acts and minutest circumstances with a sort of relish and retrospective fondness. But so near are the boundaries of panegyric and invective, that a worn-out sinner is sometimes found to make the best declaimer against sin. The same high seasoned descriptions, which in his unregenerate state served but to inflame his appetites, in his new province of a moralist will serve him, a little turned, to expose the enormity of those appetites in other men. When Cervantes with such proficiency of

fondness dwells upon the Don's library, who sees
not that he has been a great reader of books of
knight-errantry—perhaps was at some time of his
life in danger of falling into those very extravagances which he ridiculed so happily in his hero.

JOHN MARSTON

Antonio and Mellida—The situation of Andrugio
and Lucio, in the first part of this tragedy, where
Andrugio, Duke of Genoa, banished from his
country, with the loss of a son supposed drowned,
is cast upon the territory of his mortal enemy,
the Duke of Venice, with no attendants but
Lucio, an old nobleman, and a page—resembles
that of Lear and Kent in that king's distresses.
Andrugio, like Lear, manifests a kinglike impatience, a turbulent greatness, and affected resignation. The enemies which he enters lists to
combat, 'Despair and mighty Grief and sharp
Impatience,' and the forces which he brings to
vanquish them, 'cornets of horse,' etc., are in the
boldest style of allegory. They are such a 'race
of mourners' as the 'infection of sorrows loud'
in the intellect might beget on some 'pregnant
cloud' in the imagination. The prologue to the
second part, for its passionate earnestness, and
for the tragic note of preparation which it sounds,
might have preceded one of those old tales of
Thebes of Pelops' line, which Milton has so
highly commended, as free from the common

error of the poets in his day, of 'intermixing comic stuff with tragic sadness and gravity, brought in without discretion corruptly to gratify the people.' It is as solemn a preparative as the warning voice which he who saw the Apocalypse heard cry.'

What You Will.—'Oh, I shall ne'er forget how he went cloath'd,' Act I, Scene 1.—To judge of the liberality of these notions of dress, we must advert to the days of Gresham, and the consternation which a phenomenon habited like the merchant here described would have excited among the flat round caps and cloth stockings upon 'Change when those 'original arguments or tokens of a citizen's vocation were in fashion, not more for thrift and usefulness than for distinction and grace.' The blank uniformity to which all professional distinctions in apparel have been long hastening, is one instance of the decay of symbols among us, which, whether it has contributed or not to make us a more intellectual, has certainly made us a less imaginative people. Shakspeare knew the force of signs: a 'malignant and a turban'd Turk.' This 'meal-cap miller,' says the author of God's revenge against Murder, to express his indignation at an atrocious outrage committed by the miller Pierot upon the person of the fair Marieta.

AUTHOR UNKNOWN

The Merry Devil of Edmonton.—The scene in

this delightful comedy, in which Jerningham, 'with the true feeling of a zealous friend,' touches griefs of Mounchensey, seems written to make the reader happy. Few of our dramatists or nove- lists have attended enough to this. They torture and wound us abundantly. They are economists only in delight. Nothing can be finer, more gentle- manlike, and nobler, than the conversation and compliments of these young men. How delicious is Raymond Mounchensey's forgetting, in his fears, that Jerningham has a 'Saint in Essex ;' and how sweetly his friend reminds him! I wish it could be ascertained, which there is some grounds for believing, that Michael Drayton was the author of this piece. It would add a worthy appendage to the renown of that Panegyrist of my native Earth ; who has gone over her soil, in his Polyolbion, with the fidelity of a herald, and the painful love of a son; who has not left a rivulet, so narrow that it may be stept over, without honourable mention ; and has animated hills and streams with life and passion beyond the dreams of old mythology.

THOMAS HEYWOOD

A Woman Killed with Kindness.—Heywood is a sort of *prose* Shakspeare. His scenes are to the full as natural and affecting. But we miss *the poet*, that which in Shakspeare always appears out and above the surface of *the nature.* Heywood's characters in this play, for instance, his country gentlemen, etc., are exactly what we see, but of the best kind of what we see, in life. Shakspeare makes us believe, while we are among his lovely creations, that they are nothing but what we are familiar with, as in dreams new things seem old; but we awake, and sigh for the difference.

The English Traveller.—Heywood's preface to this play is interesting, as it shows the heroic indifference about the opinion of posterity, which some of these great writers seem to have felt. There is a magnanimity in authorship as in everything else. His ambition seems to have been confined to the pleasure of hearing the players speak his lines while he lived. It does not appear that he ever contemplated the possibility of being read by after ages. What a slender pittance of fame was motive sufficient to the production of such plays as the English Traveller, the Challenge for Beauty, and the Woman Killed with Kindness! Posterity is bound to take care that a writer loses nothing by such a noble modesty.

THOMAS MIDDLETON AND WILLIAM ROWLEY

A Fair Quarrel.—The insipid levelling morality to which the modern stage is tied down, would not admit of such admirable passions as these scenes are filled with. A puritanical obtuseness of sentiment, a stupid infantile goodness, is creeping among us, instead of the vigorous passions, and virtues clad in flesh and blood,

with which the old dramatists present us. Those
noble and liberal casuists could discern in the
differences, the quarrels, the animosities of men,
a beauty and truth of moral feeling, no less
than in the everlastingly inculcated duties of
forgiveness and atonement. With us, all is
hypocritical meekness. A reconciliation scene
be the occasion never so absurd, never fails of
applause. Our audiences come to the theatre
to be complimented on their goodness. They
compare notes with the amiable characters in
the play, and find a wonderful sympathy of
disposition between them. We have a common
stock of dramatic morality, out of which a
writer may be supplied without the trouble of
copying it from originals within his own breast.
To know the boundaries of honour, to be
judiciously valiant, to have a temperance which
shall beget a smoothness in the angry swellings
of youth, to esteem life as nothing when the
sacred reputation of a parent is to be defended,
yet to shake and tremble under a pious cowardice
when that ark of an honest confidence is found
to be frail and tottering; to feel the true blows
of a real disgrace blunting that sword which
the imaginary strokes of a supposed false imputa-
tion had put so keen an edge upon but lately;
to do, or to imagine this done in a feigned story
asks something more of a moral sense, somewhat a greater delicacy of perception in questions
of right and wrong, than goes to the writing of

two or three hackneyed sentences about the laws of honour as opposed to the laws of the land, or a commonplace against duelling. Yet such things would stand a writer now-a-days in far better stead than Captain Agar and his conscientious honour, and he would be considered as a far better teacher of morality than old Rowley or Middleton, if they were living.

WILLIAM ROWLEY

A New Wonder: A Woman Never Vext.—The old play-writers are distinguished by an honest boldness of exhibition, they show everything without being ashamed. If a reverse in fortune is to be exhibited, they fairly bring us to the prison grate and the alms basket. A poor man on our stage is always a gentleman, he may be known by a peculiar neatness of apparel, and by wearing black. Our delicacy in fact forbids the dramatizing of distress at all. It is never shown in its essential properties; it appears but as the adjunct of some virtue, as something which is to be relieved, from the approbation of which relief the spectators are to derive a certain soothing of self-referred satisfaction. We turn away from the real essences of things to hunt after their relative shadows, moral duties; whereas, if the truth of things were fairly represented, the relative duties might be safely trusted to

H

themselves, the moral philosophy lose the name of a science.

The Witch.—Though some resemblance may be traced between the charms in Macbeth, and the incantations in this play, which is supposed to have preceded it, this coincidence will not detract much from the originality of Shakspeare. His witches are distinguished from the witches of Middleton by essential differences. These are creatures to whom man or woman, plotting some dire mischief, might resort for occasional consultation. Those originate deeds of blood, and begin bad impulses to men. From the moment that their eyes first meet with Macbeth's, he is spell-bound. That meeting sways his destiny. He can never break the fascination. These witches can hurt the body, those have power over the soul. Hecate in Middleton has a son, a low buffoon, the hags of Shakspeare have neither child of their own, nor seem to be descended from any parent. They are foul anomalies, of whom we know not whence they are sprung, nor whether they have beginning or ending. As they are without human passions, so they seem to be without human relations. They come with thunder and lightning, and vanish to airy music. This is all we know of them. Except Hecate, they have no *names;* which heightens their mysterious-

ness. The names, and some of the properties
which the other author has given to his hags,
excite smiles. The Weird Sisters are serious
things. Their presence cannot co-exist with
mirth. But, in a lesser degree, the witches of
Middleton are fine creations. Their power too
is, in some measure, over the mind. They raise
jars, jealousies, strifes, 'like a thick scurf' over
life.

WILLIAM ROWLEY, THOMAS DECKER, JOHN FORD, ETC.

The Witch of Edmonton.—Mother Sawyer, in
this wild play, differs from the hags of both
Middleton and Shakspeare. She is the plain
traditional old woman witch of our ancestors;
poor, deformed, and ignorant; the terror of villages,
herself amenable to a justice. That should be
a hardy sheriff, with the power of the county
at his heels, that would lay hands upon the
Weird Sisters. They are of another jurisdiction.
But upon the common and received opinion, the
author (or authors) have engrafted strong fancy.
There is something frightfully earnest in her
invocations to the Familiar.

CYRIL TOURNEUR

The Revengers' Tragedy.—The reality and life of
the dialogue, in which Vindici and Hippolito first

tempt their mother, and then threaten her with
death for consenting to the dishonour of their sister,
passes any senical illusion I ever felt. I never
read it but my ears tingle, and I feel a hot blush
over-spread my cheeks, as if I were presently about
to proclaim such malefactions of myself as the
brothers here rebuke in their unnatural parent,
in words more keen and dagger-like than those
which Hamlet speaks to his mother.   Such power
has the passion of shame truly personated, not
only to strike guilty creatures unto the soul, but
to ' appal ' even those who are ' free.'

JOHN WEBSTER

The Duchess of Malfy.—All the several parts of
the dreadful apparatus with which the death of
the Duchess is ushered in, the waxen images
which counterfeit death, the wild masque of mad-
men, the tomb-maker, the bellman, the living
person's dirge, the mortification by degrees,—are
not more remote from the conceptions of ordinary
vengeance than the strange character of suffering
which they seem to bring upon their victim is out
of the imagination of ordinary poets. As they are
not like inflictions of this life, so her language
seems not of this world.   She has lived among
horrors till she is become ' native and endowed
unto that element.' She speaks the dialect of despair ; her tongue has a smatch of Tartarus and the
souls in Bale.   To move a horror skilfully, to touch

a soul to the quick, to lay upon fear as much as it can bear, to wean and weary a life till it is ready to drop, and then step in with mortal instruments to take its last forfeit : this only a Webster can do. Inferior geniuses may ' upon horror's head horrors accumulate,' but they cannot do this. They mistake quantity for quality ; they 'terrify babes with painted devils ; ' but they know not how a soul is to be moved. Their terrors want dignity, their affrightments are without decorum.

The White Devil, or Vittoria Corrombona.—This White Devil of Italy sets off a bad cause so speciously, and pleads with such an innocence-resembling boldness, that we seem to see that matchless beauty of her face which inspires such gay confidence into her, and are ready to expect, when she has done her pleadings, that her very judges, her accusers, the grave ambassadors who sit as spectators, and all the court, will rise and make proffer to defend her in spite of the utmost conviction of her guilt ; as the shepherds in Don Quixote make proffer to follow the beautiful shepherdess of Mercela, 'without making any profit of her manifest resolution made there in their hearing.'

> 'So sweet and lovely does she make the shame,
> Which, like a canker in the fragrant rose,
> Does spot the beauty of her budding name.'

I never saw anything like the funeral dirge in this play, for the death of Marcello, except the ditty which reminds Ferdinand of his drowned father in the Tempest. As that is of the water, watery; so this is of the earth, earthy. Both have that intenseness of feeling which seems to resolve itself into the element which it contemplates.

In a note on the Spanish Tragedy in the Specimens, I have said that there is nothing in the undoubted plays of Jonson, which would authorise us to suppose that he could have supplied the additions to Hieronymo. I suspected the agency of some more potent spirit. I thought that Webster might have furnished them. They seem full of that wild, solemn, preternatural cast of grief which bewilders us in the 'Duchess of Malfy.' On second consideration, I think this a hasty criticism. They are more like the overflowing griefs and talking distraction of Titus Andronicus. The sorrows of the Duchess set inward; if she talks, it is little more than soliloquy imitating conversation in a kind of bravery.

JOHN FORD

The Broken Heart.—I do not know where to find, in any play, a catastrophe so grand, so solemn, and so surprising as in this. This is indeed, according to Milton, to describe high passions and high actions. The fortitude of the Spartan boy, who let a beast gnaw out his bowls till he died without expressing a groan, is a faint bodily image of this dilaceration of the spirit, and exenteration of the

inmost mind, which Calantha, with a holy violence
against her nature, keeps closely covered, till the
last duties of a wife and a queen are fulfilled.
Stories of martyrdom are but of chains and the
stake; a little bodily suffering. These torments—

> 'On the purest spirits prey
> As on entrails, joints, and limbs,
> With answerable pains, but more intense.

What a noble thing is the soul in its strengths and
in its weaknesses! Who would be less weak than
Calantha? Who can be so strong? The expression of this transcendent scene almost bears us in
imagination to Calvary and the Cross; and we
seem to perceive some analogy between the scenical
sufferings, which we are here contemplating, and
the real agonies of that final completion to which
we dare no more than hint a reference. Ford was
of the first order of poets. He sought for sub-
limity, not by parcels, in metaphors or visible
images, but directly where she has her full
residence in the heart of man; in the actions
and sufferings of the greatest minds. There is
a grandeur of the soul above mountains, seas, and
the elements. Even in the poor perverted reason
of Giovanni and Annabella, in the play * which
stands at the head of the modern collection of
the works of this author, we discern traces of
that fiery particle, which, in the irregular starting
from out the road of beaten action, discovers

* 'Tis a pity she is a Whore.

something of a right line even in obliquity, and shows hints of an improvable greatness in the lowest descents and degradations of our nature.

FULKE GREVILLE, LORD BROOKE

Alahan, Mustapha.—The two tragedies of Lord Brooke, printed among his poems, might with more propriety have been termed political treatises than plays. Their author has strangely contrived to make passion, character, and interest, of the highest order, subservient to the expression of state dogmas and mysteries. He is nine parts Machiavel and Tacitus, for one part Sophocles or Seneca. In this writer's estimate of the powers of the mind, the understanding must have held a most tyrannical pre-eminence. Whether we look into his plays, or his most passionate love poems, we shall find all frozen and made rigid with intellect. The finest movements of the human heart, the utmost grand-eur of which the soul is capable, are essentially comprised in the actions and speeches of Cælica and Camena. Shakspeare, who seems to have had a peculiar delight in contemplating womanly per-fection, whom for his many sweet images of female excellence all women are in an especial manner bound to love, has not raised the ideal of the female character higher than Lord Brooke, in these two women, has done. But it requires a study equiva-lent to the learning of a new language to understand their meaning when they speak. It is indeed hard to hit:

> Much like thy riddle, Samson, in one day
> Or seven though one should musing sit.

It is as if a being of pure intellect should take upon him to express the emotions of our sensitive natures. There would be all knowledge, but sympathetic expressions would be wanting.

BEN JONSON

The Case is Altered.—The passion for wealth has worn out much of its grossness in tract of time. Our ancestors certainly conceived of money as able to confer a distinct gratification in itself, not considered simply as a symbol of wealth. The old poets, when they introduce a miser, make him address his gold as his mistress; as something to be seen, felt, and hugged; as capable of satisfying two of the senses at least. The substitution of a thin, unsatisfying medium in the place of the good old tangible metal, has made avarice quite a Platonic affection in comparison with the seeing, touching, and handling-pleasure of the old Chrysophilites. A bank-note can no more satisfy the touch of a true sensualist in this passion than Creusa could return her husband's embrace in the shades. See the Cave of Mammon in Spencer; Barabas's contemplation of his wealth in the Rich Jew of

Malta; Luke's raptures in the City Madam; the
idolatry and absolute gold-worship of the miser
Jaques in this early comic production of Ben
Jonson's. Above all, hear Guzman, in that excellent old translation of the Spanish Rogue, expatiate
on the 'ruddy cheeks of your golden ruddocks,
your Spanish pistolets, your plump and full-faced
Portuguese, and your clear-skined pieces of eight
of Castile,' which he and his fellows the beggars
kept secret to themselves, and did privately enjoy
in a plentiful manner. 'For to have them, to pay
them away, is not to enjoy them; to enjoy them is
to have them lying by us; having no other need of
them than to use them for the clearing of the eye-
sight, and the comforting of our senses. These we
did carry about with us, sewing them in some
patches of our doublets near unto the heart, and as
close to the skin as we could handsomely quilt them
in, holding them to be restorative.'

Poetaster.—This Roman play seems written to
confute those enemies of Ben in his own days and
ours, who have said that he made a pedantical use
of his learning. He has here revived the whole
Court of Augustus by a learned spell. We are
admitted to the society of the illustrious dead.
Virgil, Horace, Ovid, Tibullus, converse in our own
tongue more finely and poetically than they were
used to express themselves in their native Latin.
Nothing can be imagined more elegant, refined, and
court-like than the scenes between this Louis the
Fourteenth of antiquity and his literati. The

whole essence and secret of that kind of intercourse
is contained therein. The economical liberality by
which greatness, seeming to waive some part of its
prerogative, takes care to lose none of the essentials ; the prudential liberties of an inferior, which
flatter by commanded boldness and soothe with
complimentary sincerity: these, and a thousand
beautiful passages from his New Inn, his Cynthia's
Revels, and from those numerous court-masques
and entertainments which he was in the daily habit
of furnishing, might be adduced to shew the
poetical fancy and elegance of mind of the supposed rugged old bard

Alchemist.—The judgment is perfectly overwhelmed by the torrent of images, words, and
book-knowledge, with which Epicure Mammon
(Act II, Scene 2.) confounds and stuns his in-
credulous hearer. They come pouring out like the
successive falls of Nilus. They 'doubly redouble
strokes upon the foe.' Description outstrides
proof. We are made to believe effects before we
have testimony for their causes. If there be no
one image which attains the height of the sublime,
yet the confluence and assemblage of them all produce a result equal to the grandest poetry. The
huge Xerxean army countervails against single
Achilles. Epicure Mammon is the most determined
offspring of its author. It has the whole 'matter
and copy of the father—eye, nose, lip, the trick of
his frown.' It is just such a swaggerer as contemporaries have described old Ben to be. Meercraft,

Bobadil, the Host of the New Inn, have all his image and superscription. But Mammon is arrogant pretension personified. Sir Samson Legend, in Love for Love, is such another lying, overbearing character, but he does not come up to Epicure Mammon. What a ' towering bravery ' there is in his sensuality ! he affects no pleasure under a Sultan. It is as if ' Egypt with Assyria strove in luxury.'

GEORGE CHAPMAN

Bussy D' Ambois, Byron's Conspiracy, Byron's Tragedy, etc., etc.—Webster has happily character-ised the ' full and heightened style ' of Chapman, who, of all the English playwriters, perhaps approaches nearest to Shakspeare in the de-scriptive and didactic, in passages which are less purely dramatic. He could not go out of himself, as Shakspeare could shift at pleasure to inform and animate other existences, but in himself he had an eye to perceive and a soul to embrace all forms and modes of being. He would have made a great epic poet, if indeed he has not abundantly shown himself to be one; for his Homer is not so properly a translation as the stories of Achilles and Ulysses re-written. The earnestness and passion which he has put into every part of these poems, would be incredible to a reader of mere modern translations. His almost

Greek zeal for the glory of his heroes can only be
paralleled by that fierce spirit of Hebrew bigotry,
with which Milton, as if personating one of the
zealots of the old law, clothed himself when he sat
down to paint the acts of Samson against the un-
circumcised. The great obstacle to Chapman's
translations being read, is their unconquerable
quaintness. He pours out in the same breath the
most just and natural, and the most violent and
crude expressions. He seems to grasp at whatever
words come first to hand while the enthusiasm is
upon him, as if all other must be inadequate to
the divine meaning. But passion (the all in all in
poetry) is every where present, raising the low,
dignifying the mean, and putting sense into the
absurd. He makes his readers glow, weep, tremble,
take any affection which he pleases, be moved
by words, or, in spite of them, be disgusted and
overcome their disgust.

FRANCIS BEAUMONT—JOHN FLETCHER

Maid's Tragedy.—One characteristic of the excellent old poets is, their being able to bestow grace
upon subjects which naturally do not seem suscept-
ible of any. I will mention two instances. Zelmane in the Arcadia of Sidney, and Helena in the
All's Well that Ends Well of Shakspeare. What
can be more unpromising at first sight than the
idea of a young man disguising himself in woman's

attire, and passing himself off for a woman among
women; and that for a long space of time? Yet
Sir Philip has preserved so matchless a decorum,
that neither does Pyrocles' manhood suffer any
stain from the effeminacy of Zelmane, nor is the
respect due to the princesses at all diminished when
the deception comes to be known. In the sweetly
constituted mind of Sir Philip Sidney, it seems as
if no ugly thought or unhandsome meditation could
find a harbour. He turned all that he touched into
images of honour and virtue. Helena in Shakspeare is a young woman seeking a man in marriage.
The ordinary rules of courtship are reversed, the
habitual feelings are crossed. Yet with such
exquisite address this dangerous subject is handled,
that Helena's forwardness loses her no honour;
delicacy dispenses with its laws in her favour, and
nature, in her single case, seems content to suffer a
sweet violation. Aspatia, in the Maid's Tragedy,
is a character equally difficult with Helena, of
being managed with grace. She, too, is a slighted
woman, refused by the man who had once engaged
to marry her. Yet it is so artfully contrived, that
while we pity we respect her, and she descends
without degradation. Such wonders true poetry
and passion can do, to confer dignity upon subjects
which do not seem capable of it. But Aspatia
must not be compared at all points with Helena;
she does not so absolutely predominate over her
situation, but she suffers some diminution, some
abatement of the full lustre of the female character,

which Helena never does. Her character has many
degrees of sweetness, some of delicacy; but it has
weakness, which, if we do not despise, we are sorry
for. After all, Beaumont and Fletcher were but an
inferior sort of Shakspeares and Sidneys.

Philaster.—The character of Bellario must have
been extremely popular in its day. For many
years after the date of Philaster's first exhibition
on the stage, scarce a play can be found without
one of these women pages in it, following in the
train of some pre-engaged lover, calling on the
gods to bless her happy rival (his mistress), whom
no doubt she secretly curses in her heart, giving
rise to many pretty *equivoques* by the way on the
confusion of sex, and either made happy at last by
some surprising turn of fate, or dismissed with the
joint pity of the lovers and the audience. Donne
has a copy of verses to his mistress, dissuading her
from a resolution which she seems to have taken
up from some of these scenical representations,
of following him abroad as a page. It is so
earnest, so weighty, so rich in poetry, in sense,
in wit, and pathos, that it deserves to be read
as a solemn close in future to all such sickly
fancies as he there deprecates.

JOHN FLETCHER

Thierry and Theodoret.—The scene where Ordella
offers her life a sacrifice, that the King of France

may not be childless, I have always considered
as the finest in all Fletcher, and Ordella to be
the most perfect notion of the female heroic
character, next to Calantha in the Broken Heart.
She is a piece of sainted nature. Yet noble as
the whole passage is, it must be confessed that
the manner of it, compared with Shakspeare's
finest scenes, is faint and languid. Its motion
is circular not progressive. Each line resolves on
itself in a sort of separate orbit. They do not join
into one another like a running hand. Fletcher's
ideas moved slow; his versification though sweet
is tedious, it stops at every turn; he lays line upon
line, making up one after the other, adding image
to image so deliberately, that we see their junc-
tures. Shakspeare mingles everything, runs line
into line, embarrasses sentences and metaphors;
before one idea has burst its shell, another is
hatched and clamorous for disclosure. Another
striking difference between Fletcher and Shakspeare, is the fondness of the former for unnatural
and violent situations. He seems to have thought
that nothing great could be produced in an
ordinary way, the chief incidents in some of his
most admired tragedies show this.* Shakspeare
had nothing of this contortion in his mind, none of
that craving after violent situations, and flights of
strained and improbable virtue, which I think
always betrays an imperfect moral sensibility.

* Wife for a Month, Cupid's Revenge, Double Marriage, &c.

The wit of Fletcher is excellent* like his serious scenes, but there is something strained and far-fetched in both. He is too mistrustful of Nature, he always goes a little on one side of her. Shakspeare chose her without a reserve, and had riches, power, understanding, and length of days with her for a dowry.

Faithful Shepherdess.—If all the parts of this delightful pastoral had been in unison with its many innocent scenes and sweet lyric intermixtures it had been a poem fit to vie with Comus or the Arcadia, to have been put into the hands of boys and virgins, to have made matter for young dreams, like the loves of Hermia and Lysander. But a spot is on the face of this Diana. Nothing short of infatuation could have driven Fletcher upon mixing with this 'blessedness' such an ugly deformity as Chloe, the wanton shepherdess! If Chloe was meant to set off Clorin by contrast, Fletcher should have known that such weeds, by juxtaposition, do not set off, but kill sweet flowers.

PHILIP MASSINGER—THOMAS DECKER

The Virgin Martyr. — This play has some beauties of so very high an order, that with all my respect for Massinger, I do not think he had

* Without Money, and his comedies generally.

I

poetical enthusiasm capable of rising up to them. His associate Decker, who wrote old Fortunatus, had poetry enough for anything. The very impurities which obtrude themselves among the sweet pieties of this play like Satan among the Sons of Heaven, have a strength of contrast, a raciness, and a glow in them, which are beyond Massinger. They are to the religion of the rest, what Caliban is to Miranda.

PHILIP MASSINGER—THOMAS MIDDLETON—
WILLIAM ROWLEY

Old Law.—There is an exquisiteness of moral sensibility, making one's eyes to gush out tears of delight, and a poetical strangeness in the circumstances of this sweet tragi-comedy, which are unlike anything in the dramas which Massinger wrote alone. The pathos is of a subtler edge. Middleton and Rowley, who assisted in it, had both of them finer geniuses than their associate.

JAMES SHIRLEY

Claims a place amongst the worthiest of this period, not so much from any transcendent talent in himself, as that he was the last of a great race, all of whom spoke nearly the same language, and had a set of moral feelings and notions in common. A new language, and quite a new turn of tragic and comic interest came in with the Restoration.

IT is praise of Shakspeare, with reference to the play-writers, his contemporaries, that he has so few revolting characters. Yet he has one that is singularly mean and disagreeable—the King in Hamlet. Neither has he characters of insignificance, unless the phantom that stalks over the stage as Julius Cæsar, in the play of that name, may be accounted one. Neither has he envious characters, excepting the short part of Don John, in Much Ado About Nothing. Neither has he unentertaining characters, if we except Parolles, and the little there is of the Clown, in All's Well That Ends Well.

It would settle the dispute, as to whether Shakspeare intended Othello for a jealous character, to consider how differently we are affected towards him, and for Leontes in the Winter's Tale. Leontes *is* that character. Othello's fault was simply credulity.

Is it possible that Shakspeare should never have read Homer, in Chapman's version at least? If he had read it, could he mean to *travesty* it in the parts of those big boobies, Ajax and Achilles? Ulysses, Nestor, Agamemnon, are true to their parts in the Iliad: they are gentlemen at least. Thersites, though unamusing, is fairly deducible from it. Troilus and Cressida are a fine graft upon it. But those two big bulks!

Lear. Who are you?
Mine eyes are none o' the best. I'll tell you straight.
Are you not Kent?
Kent. The same; your servant, Kent.
Where is your servant, Caius?
Lear. He's a good fellow, I can tell you that;
He'd strike, and quickly too: he's dead and rotten.
Kent. No, my good Lord; I am the very man—
Lear. I'll see that straight—
Kent. That, from your first of difference and decay,
Have follow'd your sad steps.
Lear. You are welcome hither.
Albany. He knows not what he says; and vain it is
That we present us to him.
Edgar. Look up, my Lord.
Kent. Vex not his ghost. O, let him pass! He hates him,
That would upon the rack of this tough world
Stretch him out longer.

So ends King Lear, the most stupendous of the Shakspearian dramas; and Kent, the noblest feature of the conceptions of his divine mind. This is the magnanimity of authorship, when a writer, having a topic presented to him, fruitful of beauties for common minds, waives his privilege, and trusts to the judicious few for understanding the reason of his abstinence. What a pudder would a common dramatist have raised here of a reconciliation scene, a perfect recognition, between the assumed Caius and his master!—to the suffusing of many fair eyes, and the moistening of cambric handkerchiefs. The old dying king partially catching at the truth, and immediately lapsing into obliviousness, with the high-minded carelessness of the other to have his services appreciated, as one that

> ——served not for gain,
> Or follow'd out of form,

are among the most judicious, not to say heart-touching, strokes in Shakspeare.

I—AT THE OLYMPIC THEATRE

THIS theatre, fitted up with new and tasteful decorations, opened on Monday with a burletta founded, upon a pleasant extravagance recorded of Wilmot the 'Mad Lord' of Rochester. The house, in its renovated condition, is just what playhouses should be, and once were; from its size admirably adapted for seeing and hearing, and only perhaps rather too well lit up. Light is a good thing, but to preserve the eyes is still better. Elliston and Mrs Edwin personated a reigning wit and beauty of the Court of Charles the Second to the life. But the charm of the evening to us, we confess, was the acting of Mrs T. Gould (late Miss Burrell) in the burlesque

Don Giovanni, which followed. This admirable piece of foolery takes up our hero just where the legitimate drama leaves him, on the 'burning marl.' We are presented with a fair map of Tartarus, the triple-headed cur, the Furies, the Tormentors, and the Don, prostrate, thunder-smitten. But there is an elasticity in the original make of this *strange man*, as Richardson would have called him. He is not of those who change with the change of climate. He brings with him to his new habitation *ardours* as glowing and constant as those he finds there. No sooner is he recovered from his first surprise than he falls to his old trade, is caught 'ogling *Proserpine*,' and coquets with two she-devils at once, till he makes the house *too hot to hold him;* and *Pluto* (in whom a wise jealously seems to produce the effects of kindness) turns him neck and heels out of his dominions—much to the satisfaction of *Giovanni*, who, stealing a boat from *Charon*, and a pair of light heels from *Mercury*, or (as he familiarly terms him) *Murky*, sets off with flying colours, conveying to the world above the souls of three damsels, just eloped from *Styx*, to comfort his tender and new-born spiritualities on the journey. Arrived upon earth (with a new body, we are to suppose, but his old habits), he lights *apropos* upon a tavern in London, at the door of which three merry weavers, widowers, are trolling a catch in triumph over their deceased spouses—

'They lie in yonder churchyard
At rest—and so are we.'

Their departed partners prove to be the identical lady ghosts who have accompanied the Don in his flight, whom he now delivers up in perfect health and good plight, not a jot the worse for their journey, to the infinite surprise and consternation, ill-dis- sembled, of their ill-fated, twice-yoked mates. The gallantries of the Don in his second state of probation, his meeting with *Leporello*, with *Donna Anna*, and a countless host of injured virgins besides, doing penance in the humble occupation of apple-women, fish-wives, and sausage-fryers, in the purlieus of Billingsgate and Covent Garden, down to the period of his complete reformation, and being made an honest man of, by marrying into a sober English citizen's family, although infinitely pleasant in the exhibition, would be somewhat tedious in the recital; but something must be said of his representative.

We have seen Mrs Jordan in male characters, and more ladies besides than we would wish to recollect—but never any that so completely an- swered the purpose for the mock of *Giovanni*. This part, as it is played at the Great House in the Haymarket (shade of Mozart, and ye living admirers of *Ambrogetti*, pardon the barbarity) had always something repulsive and distasteful to us. We cannot sympathise with *Leporello's* brutal dis- play of the *list*, and were shocked (not strait-laced moralists either) with the applauses, with the *endurance* we ought rather to say, which fashion and beauty bestowed upon that disgustful insult to femine unhappiness. The *Leporello* of the Olympic Theatre is not of the most refined order; but we can bear with an English blackguard better than with the hard Italian. But *Giovanni*—free, fine, frank-spirted, single-hearted creature, turning all the mischief into fun as harmless as toys or children's *make-believe*, what praise can we repay to you, adequate to the pleasure which you have given us? We had better be silent, for you have no names, and our mention may be thought fantastical. You have taken out the sting from the evil thing, but by what magic we know not; for there are actresses of greater mark and attributes than you. With you and your *Giovanni* our spirits will hold communion whenever sorrow or suffering shall be our lot. We have seen you triumph over the infernal powers; and pain, and Erebus, and the powers of darkness are henceforth ' Shapes of a dream.'

II—MISS KELLY AT BATH

Extract of a letter to the Editor of the ' Examiner,' from an old correspondent in London.

DEAR G——, I was thinking yesterday of our old play-going days, of your and my partiality to Mrs Jordan, of our disputes as to the relative merits of Dodd and Parsons, and whether Smith or Jack Palmer were the most of a gentleman. The occasion of my falling into this train of thinking, was my learning from the newspapers that Miss Kelly is paying the Bath Theatre a visit (your own theatre, I am sorry to find, is shut up, either from parsimonious feelings, or through the influence of ———— principles).* This lady has long ranked among the most considerable of our London performers. If there are one or two of greater name, I must impute it to the circumstance that she has never burst upon the town at once in the maturity of her powers, which is a great advantage to *debutantes* who have passed their probationary years in Provincial Theatres. We do not hear them tuning their instruments. But she has been winning her patient way from the humblest degradations to the eminence which she has now attained, on the self same - boards which supported her first in the slender pretensions of chorus singer. I very much wish you would go and see her. You will not see Mrs Jordan, but something else ; something on the whole very little, if at all, inferior to that lady in her best days. I cannot hope that you will think so, I do not even wish that you should. Our longest remembrances are the most sacred, and I shall revere the prejudice that shall prevent you from thinking quite so favourably of her as I do. I do not well know how to draw a parallel between their distinct manners of acting. I seem to recognise the same pleasantness and nature in both. But Mrs Jordan's was the carelessness of a child ; her childlike spirit

---

* The word here omitted by the Bristol editor, we suppose, is Methodistical.

shook off the load of years from her spectators; she seemed one whom care could not come near; a privileged being sent to teach mankind what he most wants—joyousness. Hence, if we had more unmixed pleasure from her performances, we had perhaps less sympathy with them than with those of her successor. This latter lady's is the joy of a freed spirit escaping from care, as a bird that had been limed; her smiles, if I may use the expression, seemed saved out of the fire, relics which a good spirit had snatched up as most portable; her discontents are visitors and not inmates; she can lay them by altogether, and when she does so, I am not sure that she is not greatest. She is in truth no ordinary tragedian. Her Yarico is the most intense piece of acting which I ever witnessed, the most heart-rending spectacle. To see her leaning upon that wretched reed, her lover—the very exhibition of whose character would be a moral offence, but for her clinging and noble credulity—to see her lean upon that flint, and by the strong workings of passion, imagine it a god, is one of the most afflicting lessons of the yearnings of the human heart and its mistakes, that was ever read upon a stage. The whole performance is everywhere African, fervid, glowing. Nor is this anything more than the wonderful force of imagination in this performer; for turn but the scene, and you shall have her come forward in some kindly home-drawn character of an English rustic, a Phœbe, or a Dinah Cropley where you would swear that her thoughts

had never strayed beyond the precincts of the dairy
or the farm, or her mind known less tranquil passions than she might have learned among the flock,
her out-of-door companions. See her again in parts
of pure fun, such as the Housemaid in the Merry
Mourners, where the suspension of the broom in
her hand, which she has been delightfully twirling,
on unexpectedly encountering her sweetheart in the
character of her fellow-servant, is quite equal to
Mrs Jordan's cordial inebriation in Nell. I do not
know whether I am not speaking it to her honour,
that she does not succeed in what are called fine
lady parts. Our friend C—— once observed that
no man of genius ever figured as a gentleman.
Neither did any woman gifted with Mrs Jordan's
or Miss Kelly's sensibilities ever take upon herself
to shine as a fine lady; the very essence of this
character consisting in the entire repression of all
genius and all feeling. To sustain a part of this
kind to the life, a performer must be haunted by a
perpetual self-reference, she must be always thinking of herself, and how she looks, and how she
deports herself in the eyes of the spectators;
whereas the delight of actresses of true feeling and
of real power, is to elude the personal notice of
an audience, to escape into their parts and hide
themselves under the hood of their assumed
character. Their most self-possession is in fact a
self-forgetfulness; an oblivion alike of self and
spectators. For this reason your most approved
epilogue-speakers have been always ladies who

have possessed least of this self-forgetting quality;
and I think I have seen the amiable actress in
question suffering some embarrassment, when she
has had an address of the sort to deliver; when she
found the modest veil of personation, which had
half-hid her from the audience, suddenly withdrawn, and herself brought without any such
gratifying intervention before the public.

I would apologise for the length of this letter, if
I did not remember the lively interest you used to
take in theatrical performers.

I am, &c., &c.

Feb. 7, 1819.   ₒ ₒ ₒ ₒ

III—'THE JOVIAL CREW'

THE *Jovial Crew*, or the *Merry Beggars*, has been
revived here [at the English Opera] after an
interval, as the bills tell us, of seven years. Can it
be so long (it seems but yesterday) since we saw
poor Lovegrove in Justice Clack? His childish
treble still pipes in our ears; 'Whip 'em, whip 'em,
whip 'em.' Dowton was the representative of the
Justice the other night, and shook our ribs most
incontinently. He was in 'excellent foolery,' and
our lungs crowed chanticleer. Yet it appears to us
that there was a still higher strain of fatuity in his
predecessor—that his eyes distilled a richer dotage.
Perhaps, after all, it was an error of the memory.
Defunct merit comes out upon us strangely.

Easy natural Wrench was the Springlove; too

comfortable a personage perhaps to personify
Springlove, in whom the voice of the bird awakens
a restless instinct of roaming that had slept during
the winter. Miss Stevenson certainly leaves us
nothing to regret for the absence of the lady, however agreeable, who formerly performed the part of
Meriel. Miss Stevenson is a fine open-countenanced
lass, with glorious girlish manners. But the
Princess of Mumpers, and Lady Paramount of
beggarly counterfeit accents, was *she* that played
Rachel. Her gabbling lachrymose petitions; her
tones, such as we have heard by the side of old
woods, when an irresistible face has come peeping
on one on a sudden; with her full black locks, and
a *voice*—how shall we describe it ?—a voice that
was by nature meant to convey nothing but truth
and goodness, but warped by circumstance into an
assurance that she is telling us a lie—that catching
twitch of the thievish irreprovable finger—those
ballad-singers' notes, so vulgar, yet so unvulgar—
that assurance so like impudence and yet so many
countless leagues removed from it—her jeers, which
we had rather stand, than be caressed with other
ladies' compliments, a summer's day long—her face,
with a wild out-of-doors grace upon it—

Altogether, a brace of more romantic she-beggars
it was never our fortune to meet in this supplicatory
world. The youngest might have sat for ' pretty
Bessy,' whose father was an Earl, and whose legend
still adorns the front of mine hostess's doors at

Bethnal Green ; and the other could be no less than the ' Beggar Maid' whom ' King Cophetua wooed.'

' What a lass that were,' said a stranger who sate beside us, speaking of Miss Kelly, in Rachel, ' to go a-gipsying through the world with.' We confess we longed to drop a tester in her lap, she begged so masterly.

By-the-way, this is the true *Beggar's Opera*. The other should have been called the *Mirror for Highwaymen*. We wonder the Societies for the Suppression of Mendicity (and other good things) do not club for the putting down of this infamous protest in favour of air, and clear liberty, and honest license, and blameless assertion of man's original blest charter of blue skies, and vagrancy, and nothing-to-do.

July 4, 1819.

IV—' THE HYPOCRITE '

By one of those perversions which actuate poor mortals in the place of motives (to persuade us into the notion that we are free agents, we presume), we had never till the other evening seen Dowton [at the English Opera] in Dr Cantwell. By a pious fraud of Mr Arnold's, who by a process as simple as some of those by which Mathews metamorphoses his person, has converted the play into an opera— a conversion, by-the-way, for which we are deeply indebted to him—we have been favoured with this rich novelty at our favourite theatre. It seems

a little unreasonable to come lagging in with a
posthumous testimony to the merits of a performance of which the town has long rung, but we
cannot help remarking in Mr Dowton's acting, the
subtle *gradations* of the hypocrisy; the length to
which it runs in proportion as the recipient is capable of taking it in; the gross palpable way in
which he administers the dose in wholesale to old
Lady Lambert, that rich fanatic; the somewhat
more guarded manner in which he retails it out,
only so much at a time as he can bear, to the somewhat less bitten fool her son; and the almost
absence of it before the younger members of the
family, when nobody else is by; how the cloven
foot peeps out a little and a little more, till the
diabolical nature is stung out at last into full mani-
festation of its horrid self.   What a grand
insolence in the tone which he assumes, when
he commands Sir John to quit *his* house ; and then
the tortures and agonies when he is finally baffled !
It is in these last perhaps that he is greatest, and
we should be doing injustice not to compare this
part of the performance with, and in some respects
to give it the preference above, the acting of Mr
Kean, in a situation nearly analogous, at the conclusion of the *City Madam.*   Cantwell reveals his
pangs with quite as much force, and without the
assistance of those contortions which transform the
detected Luke into the similitude of a mad tiger, or
a foaming demon.   Dowton plays it neither like
beast or demon, but simply as it should be, a bold

bad man pushed to extremity. Humanity is never once overstepped. Has it ever been noticed, the exquisite modulation with which he drawls out the word 'Charles,' when he calls his secretary, so humble, so seraphic, so resigned. The most diabolical of her sex that we ever knew accented her honey devil words in just such a hymn-like smoothness. The Spirit of Whitfield seems hovering in the air, to suck the blessed tones so much like his own upon earth : Lady Huntingdon claps her neat white wings, and gives it out again in heaven to the sainted ones, in approbation.

Miss Kelly is not quite at home in Charlotte; she is too good for such parts. Her cue is to be natural; she cannot put on the modes of artificial life, and play coquette as it is expected to be played. There is a frankness in her tones which defeats her purposes; we could not help wondering why her lover (Mr Pearman) looked so rueful; we forgot that she was acting airs and graces, as she seemed to forget it herself, turning them into a playfulness which could breed no doubt for a moment which way her inclinations ran. She is in truth not framed to tease or torment even in jest, but to utter a hearty *Yes* or *No*; to yield or refuse assent with a noble sincerity. We have not the pleasure of being acquainted with her, but we have been told that she carries the same cordial manners into private life. We have heard too, of some virtues which she is in the practice of; but they are of a description

K

which repay themselves, and with them neither we nor the public have anything to do.

One word about Wrench who played the Colonel— Was this man never unhappy? It seems as if care never came near him, as if the black ox could never tread upon his foot; we want something calamitous to befall him, to bring him down to us. It is a shame he should be suffered to go about with his well-looking happy face and tones insulting us thin race of irritable and irritable-making critics.

Aug. 2, 1819.

V—NEW PIECES AT THE LYCEUM

A PLOT has broke out in this theatre. Some quarrel has been breeding between the male and female performers, and the women have determined to set up for themselves. Seven of them, *Belles without Beaux* they call themselves, have undertaken to get up a piece without any assistance from the men, and in our opinion have established their point most successfully. There is Miss Carew with her silvery tones, and Miss Stevenson with her delicious mixture of the school-girl and waiting-maid, and Miss Kelly, sure to be first in any mischief, and Mrs Chatterly, with some of the best acting we have ever witnessed, and Miss Love, worthy of the *name*, and Mrs Grove that rhymes to her, and Mrs Richardson who might in charity have been allowed somewhat a larger portion of the dialogue. The effect was enchanting. We mean for once. We do

not want to encourage these Amazonian vanities.
Once or twice we longed to have Wrench bustling
among them. A lady who sate near us was
observed to gape for want of variety. To us it
was delicate quintessence, apple-pie made all of
quinces. We remember poor Holcroft's last comedy,
which positively died from the opposite excess; it
was choked up with men, and perished from a
redundancy of male population. It had nine principal men characters in it, and but one woman, and
she of no very ambiguous character. Mrs Harlow,
to do the part justice, chose to play it in scarlet.

We did not know Mrs Chatterly's merits before
she plays with downright sterling good acting, a
prude who is to be convinced out of her prudery by
Miss Kelly's (we did not catch her stage name)
assumption of the dress and character of a brother
of seventeen, who makes the prettiest unalarming
platonic approaches; and in the shyest mark of
moral battery, no one step of which you can
detect, or say *this* is decidedly going too far,
vanquishes at last the ice of her scruples, brings
her into an infinite scrape, and then with her own
infinite good humour sets all to right, and brings
her safe out of it again with an explanation. Mrs
Chatterly's embarrassments were masterly. Miss
Stevenson her maid's start at surprising a youth in
her mistress's closet at midnight, was quite as good.
Miss Kelly we do not care to say anything about,
because we have been accused of flattering her.
The truth is, this lady puts so much intelligence

and good sense into every part which she plays, that there is no expressing an honest sense of her merits without incurring a suspicion of that sort. But what have we to gain by praising Miss Kelly? Altogether, this little feminine republic, this provoking experiment, went off most smoothly. What a nice world it would be, we sometimes think, *all women!* but then we are afraid, *we slip in a fallacy unawares into the hypothesis*; we somehow edge in the idea of ourselves as spectators or something among them.

We saw Wilkinson after it in *Walk for a Wager*. What a picture of forlorn hope! of abject orphan destitution! He seems to have no friends in the world but his legs, and he plies them accordingly. He goes walking on like a perpetual motion. His continual ambulatory presence performs the part of a Greek chorus. He is the walking gentleman of the piece; a peripatetic that would make a stoic laugh. He made us cry. Mr Muffincap in *Amateurs and Actors* is just such another piece of acting. We have seen charity boys, both of St Clement's and Farringdon. Without, looking just as old, ground down out of all semblance of youth by abject and hopeless neglect—you cannot guess their age between fifteen and fifty. If Mr Peake be the author of these pieces, he has no reason to be piqued at their reception.

We must apologise for an oversight in our last week's article. The allusion made to Mr Kean's acting of Luke in the *City Madam* was totally inapplicable to the part and to the play. We were thinking of his performance of the concluding scenes of *The New Way to Pay Old Debts*. We confounded one of Massinger's strange heroes with the other. It was Sir Giles Overreach we meant; nor are we sure that our remark was just, even with this explanation. When we consider the intense tone in which Mr Kean thinks it proper (and he is quite as likely to be in the right as his blundering critic) to pitch the temperament of that monstrous character from the beginning, it follows but logically and naturally, that where the wild uncontrollable man comes to be baffled of his purpose, his passion should assume a frenzied manner, which it was altogether absurd to expect should be the same with the manner of the cautious and self-restraining *Cantwell*, even when he breaks loose from all bonds in the agony of his final exposure. We never felt more strongly the good sense of the saying—comparisons are odious. They betray us not seldom into bitter errors of judgment; and sometimes, as in the present instance, into absolute matter-of-fact blunders. But we have recanted.

Aug. 1819.

ON the noon of the 14th of November, 1743 or 1744, I forget which it was, just as the clock had struck one, Barbara S——, with her accustomed punctuality, ascended the long rambling staircase, with awkward interposed landing-places, which led to the office, or rather a sort of box with a desk in it, whereat sat the then treasurer of (what few of our readers may remember) the old Bath Theatre. All over the island it was the custom, and remains so I believe to this day, for the players to receive their weekly stipend on the Saturday. It was not much that Barbara had to claim.

This little maid had just entered her eleventh year; but her important station at the theatre, as it seemed to her, with the benefits which she felt to accrue from her pious application of her small earnings, had given an air of womanhood to her steps and to her behaviour. You would have taken her to have been at least five years older.

Till latterly she had merely been employed in choruses, or where children were wanted to fill up the scene; but the manager, observing a diligence and adroitness in her above her age, had for some few months past entrusted to her the performance of whole parts. You may guess the self-consequence of the promoted Barbara. She had already drawn tears in young Arthur; had rallied Richard with infantine petulance in the Duke of York; and in her turn had rebuked that petulance when she was Prince of Wales. She would have done the elder child in Morton's pathetic afterpiece to the life; but as yet the 'Children in the Wood' was not.

Long after this little girl was grown an aged woman, I have seen some of these small parts each making two or three pages at most, copied out in the rudest hand of the then prompter, who doubtless transcribed a little more carefully and fairly for the grown-up tragedy ladies of the establishment. But such as they were, blotted and scrawled, as for a child's use, she kept them all; and in the zenith of her after reputation it was a delightful sight to behold them bound up in costliest morocco, each single—each small part making a *book*—with fine clasps, gilt-splashed, &c. She had conscientiously kept them as they had been delivered to her; not a blot had been effaced or tampered with. They were precious to her for their affecting remembrancings. They were her principia, her rudiments: the elementary atoms; the little steps by which she pressed forward to perfection. 'What,' she would say, 'could India-rubber, or pumice stone, have done for these darlings?'

I am in no hurry to begin my story—indeed I have little or none to tell—so I will just mention an observation of hers connected with that interesting time.

Not long before she died I had been discoursing with her on the quantity of real present emotion which a great tragic performer experiences during acting. I ventured to think, that, though in the first instance such players must have possessed the feelings which they so powerfully called up in others, yet by frequent repetition those feelings must become deadened in a great measure, and the performer trust to the memory of past emotion, rather than express a present one. She indignantly repelled the notion that, with a truly great tragedian, the operation by which such effects were produced upon an audience could ever degrade itself into what was purely mechanical. With much delicacy, avoiding to instance her *self*-experience, she told me that so long ago as when she used to play the part of the Little Son to Mrs Porter's Isabella (I think it was), when that impressive actress has been bending over her in some heart-rending colloquy, she has felt real hot tears come trickling from her, which (to use

her powerful expression) have perfectly scalded her
back.

I am not quite so sure that it was Mrs Porter;
but it was some great actress of that day. The
name is indifferent; but the fact of the scalding
tears I most distinctly remember.

I was always fond of the society of players, and
am not sure that an impediment in my speech
(which certainly kept me out of the pulpit) even
more than certain personal disqualifications, which
are often got over in that profession, did not prevent me at one time of life from adopting it. 'I
have had the honour (I must ever call it) once to
have been admitted to the tea-table of Miss Kelly.
I have played at serious whist with Mr Liston.
I have chattered with the ever good-humoured Mrs
Charles Kemble. I have conversed as friend to
friend with her accomplished husband. I have
been indulged with a classical conference with
Macready; and with a sight of the Player Picture
Gallery at Mr Mathews', when the kind owner,
to remunerate me for my love of the old actors,
(whom he loves so much) went over it with me,
supplying to his capital collection what alone the
artist could give them — voice and their living
motion. Old tones, half-faded, of Dodd, and
Parsons, and Baddeley, have lived again for me
at his bidding. Only Edwin he could not restore
to me. I have supped with ——, but I am growing a coxcomb.

As I was about to say, at the desk of the then

treasurer of the old Bath Theatre (not Diamond's) presented herself the little Barbara S——.

The parents of Barbara had been in reputable circumstances. The father had practised, I believe, as an apothecary in the town; but his practice, from causes which I feel my own infirmity too sensibly that way to arraign—or perhaps from that pure infelicity which accompanies some people in their walk through life, and which it is impossible to lay at the door of imprudence—was now reduced to nothing. They were in fact in the very teeth of starvation, when the manager, who knew and respected them in better days, took the little Barbara into his company.

At the period I commenced with, her slender earnings were the sole support of her family, including two younger sisters. I must throw a veil over some mortifying circumstances. Enough to say, that her Saturday's pittance was the only chance of a Sunday's (generally their only) meal of meat.

One thing I will only mention, that in some child's part, where in her theatrical character she was to sup off a roast fowl, (O joy to Barbara!) some comic actor, who was for the night caterer for this dainty—in the misguided humour of his part, threw over the dish such a quantity of salt (O grief and pain of heart to Barbara!) that when she crammed a portion of it into her mouth, she was obliged splutteringly to reject it; and what with shame of her ill-acted part, and pain of real appetite at missing such a dainty, her little heart sobbed almost to bursting, till a flood of tears, which the well-fed spectators were totally unable to comprehend, mercifully relieved her.

This was the little starved, meritorious maid, who stood before old Ravenscroft, the treasurer, for her Saturday's payment.

Ravenscroft was a man, I have heard many old theatrical people besides herself say, of all men least calculated for a treasurer. He had no head for accounts, paid away at random, kept scarce any books, and summing up at the week's end, if he found himself a pound or so deficient, blest himself that it was no worse.

Now Barbara's weekly stipend was a bare half-guinea. By mistake he popped into her hand a whole one.

Barbara tripped away.

She was entirely unconscious at first of the mistake: God knows, Ravenscroft would never have discovered it.

But when she had got down to the first of those uncouth landing-places, she became sensible of an unusual weight of metal pressing her left hand.

Now mark the dilemma.

She was by nature a good child. From her parents and those about her she had imbibed no contrary influence; but then they had taught her nothing. Poor men's smoky cabins are not always porticoes of moral philosophy. This little maid had no instinct to evil, but then she might be

said to have no fixed principle. She had heard
honesty commended, but never dreamed of its
application to herself. She thought of it as something which concerned grown-up people, men and
women. She had never known temptation, or
thought of preparing resistance against it.

Her first impulse was to go back to the old
treasurer, and explain to him his blunder. He was
already so confused with age, besides a natural
want of punctuality, that she would have had some
difficulty in making him understand it. She saw
that in an instant. And then it was such a bit
of money ! and then the image of a larger allowance of butcher's meat on their table next day came
across her, till her little eyes glistened, and her
mouth moistened. But then Mr Ravenscroft
had always been so good-natured, had stood her
friend behind the scenes, and even recommended
her promotion to some of her little parts. But
again the old man was reputed to be worth a world
of money : he was supposed to have fifty pounds
a year clear of the theatre. And then came staring
upon her the figures of her little stockingless
and shoeless sisters. And when she looked at
her own neat white cotton stockings, which her
situation at the theatre had made it indispensable
for her mother to provide for her, with hard strain-
ing and pinching from the family stock, and
thought how glad she would be to cover their poor
feet with the same—and how then they could
accompany her to rehearsals, which they had

hitherto been precluded from doing, by reason
of their unfashionable attire—in these thoughts
she reached the second landing-place—the second,
I mean, from the top—for there was still another
left to traverse.

Now virtue, support Barbara!

And that never-failing friend did step in; for at
that moment a strength not her own, I have heard
her say, was revealed to her—a reason above
reasoning—and without her own agency, as it
seemed (for she never felt her feet to move), she
found herself transported back to the individual
desk she had just quitted, and her hand in the old
hand of Ravenscroft, who in silence took back the
refunded treasure, and who had been sitting (good
man) insensible to the lapse of minutes, which
to her were anxious ages, and from that moment a
deep peace fell upon her heart, and she knew the
quality of honesty.

A year or two's unrepining application to her
profession brightened up the feet and the prospects
of her little sisters, set the whole family upon their
legs again, and released her from the difficulty of
discussing moral dogmas upon a landing-place.

I have heard her say that it was a surprise,
not much short of mortification to her, to see the
coolness with which the old man pocketed the
difference, which had caused her such mortal
throes.

This anecdote of herself I had in the year 1800,

from the mouth of the late Mrs Crawford,* then
sixty-seven years of age, (she died soon after);
and to her struggles upon this childish occasion I
have sometimes ventured to think her indebted for
that power of rending the heart in the representation of conflicting emotions, for which in after
years she was considered as little inferior (if at all
so in the part of Lady Randolph) even to Mrs
Siddons.

*‾ The maiden name of this lady was Street, which she changed, by
successive marriages, for those of Dancer, Barry, and Crawford. She
was Mrs Crawford, a third time a widow, when I knew her.

———

AT the north end of Cross Court there yet stands a portal, of some architectural pretensions, though reduced to humble use, serving at present for an entrance to a printing-office. This old doorway, if you are young, reader, you may not know was the identical pit-entrance to old Drury—Garrick's Drury—all of it that is left. I never pass it without shaking some forty years from off my shoulders, recurring to the evening when I passed through it to see *my first play*. The afternoon had been wet, and the condition of our going (the elder folks and myself) was, that the rain should cease. With what a beating heart did I watch from the window the puddles, from the stillness of which I

was taught to prognosticate the desired cessation
I seem to remember the last spurt, and the glee
with which I ran to announce it.

We went with orders, which my godfather F.
had sent us. He kept the oil shop (now Davies's)
at the corner of Featherstone Buildings, in Holborn.
F. was a tall, grave person, lofty in speech, and had
pretensions above his rank. He associated in those
days with John Palmer, the comedian, whose gait
and bearing he seemed to copy ; if John (which is
quite as likely) did not rather borrow somewhat of
his manner from my godfather. He was also known
to, and visited by, Sheridan. It was to his house
in Holborn that young Brinsley brought his first
wife on her elopement with him from a boarding-
school at Bath—the beautiful Maria Linley. My
parents were present (over a quadrille table) when
he arrived in the evening with his harmonious
charge. From either of these connections it may
be inferred that my godfather could command an
order for the then Drury Lane Theatre at pleasure ;
and, indeed, a pretty liberal issue of those cheap
billets, in Brinsley's easy autograph, I have heard
him say, was the sole remuneration which he had
received for many years' nightly illumination of
the orchestra and various avenues of that theatre ;
and he was content it should be so. The honour
of Sheridan's familiarity, or supposed familiarity,
was better to my godfather than money.

F. was the most gentlemanly of oilmen ; grandil-
oquent, yet courteous. His delivery of the commonest

matters of fact was Ciceronian. He had two Latin words almost constantly i.i his mouth, (how odd sounds Latin from an oilman's lips!) which my better knowledge since has enabled me to correct. In strict pronunciation they should have been sounded *vice versâ*; but in these young years they impressed me with more awe than they would do now, read aright from Seneca or Varro—in his own peculiar pronunciation, monosyllabically elaborated, or Anglicised into something like *verse verse*. By an imposing manner, and the help of these distorted syllables, he climbed (but that was little) to the highest parochial honours which St Andrew's has to bestow.

He is dead : and this much I thought due to his memory, both for my first orders (little wondrous talismans ! slight keys, and insignificant to outward sight, but opening to me more than Arabian paradises !), and, moreover, that by his testamentary beneficence I came into possession of the only landed property which I could ever call my own, situated near the road-way village of pleasant Puckeridge, in Hertfordshire. When I journeyed down to take possession, and planted foot on my own ground, the stately habits of the donor descended upon me, and I strode (shall I confess the vanity ?) with larger paces over my allotment of three-quarters of an acre, with its commodious mansion in the midst, with the feeling of an English freeholder that all betwixt sky and centre was my own. The estate has passed into more prudent hands, and nothing but an agrarian can restore it. In those days were pit orders.—Beshrew the uncomfortable manager who abolished them—with one of these we went. I remember the waiting at the door—not that which is left—but between that and an inner door in shelter. O when shall I be such an expectant again!—with the cry of nonpareils, an indispensable play-house accompaniment in those days. As near as I can recollect, the fashionable pronunciation of the theatrical fruiteresses then was, 'Chase some oranges, chase some numparls, chase a bill of the play;'—chase *pro* chuse. But when we got in, and I beheld the green curtain that veiled a heaven to my imagination, which was soon to be disclosed—the breathless anticipations I endured! I had seen something like it in the plate prefixed to *Troilus and Cressida*, in Rowe's Shakspeare—the tent-scene with Diomede; and a sight of that plate can always bring back in a measure the feeling of that evening. The boxes at that time, full of well-dressed women of quality, projected over the pit; and the pilasters reaching down were adorned with a glistering substance (I know not what) under glass (as it seemed), resembling a homely fancy, but I judged it to be sugar-candy; yet to my raised imagination, divested of its homelier qualities, it appeared a glorified candy! The orchestra lights at length arose, those 'fair Auroras!' Once the bell sounded. It was to ring out yet once again; and, incapable of the anticipation, I reposed my shut eyes in a sort of resignation upon the maternal lap. It rang the second time. The curtain drew up (I was not past six years old) and the play was *Artaxerxes !*

I had dabbled a little in the *Universal History*—the ancient part of it—and here was the court of Persia. It was being admitted to a sight of the past. I took no proper interest in the action going on, for I understood not its import; but I heard the word Darius, and I was in the midst of Daniel. All feeling was absorbed in vision. Gorgeous vests, gardens, palaces, princesses, passed before me. I knew not players. I was in Persepolis for the time, and the burning idol of their devotion almost converted me into a worshipper. I was awe-struck, and believed those significations to be something more than elemental fires. It was all enchantment and a dream. No such pleasure has since visited me but in dreams. Harlequin's invasion followed; where, I remember, the transformation of the magistrates into reverend beldams seemed to me a piece of grave historic justice, and the tailor carrying his own head to be as sober a verity as the legend of St Denys.

The next play to which I was taken was the *Lady of the Manor*; of which, with the exception of some scenery, very faint traces are left in my memory. It was followed by a pantomime, called *Lun's Ghost*—a satiric touch, I apprehend, upon Rich, not long since dead—but to my apprehension (too sincere for satire) Lun was as remote a piece of

antiquity as Lud—the father of a line of Harlequins
—transmitting his dagger of lath (the wooden
sceptre) through countless ages. I saw the
primeval Motley come from his silent tomb in a
ghastly vest of white patchwork, like the apparition
of a dead rainbow. So Harlequins (thought I) look
when they are dead.

My third play followed in quick succession. It
was the *Way of the World.* I think I must have
sat at it as grave as a judge; for I remember
the hysteric affectations of good Lady Wishfort
affected me like some solemn tragic passion.
Robinson Crusoe followed; in which Crusoe's man,
Friday, and the parrot were as good and authentic
as in the story. The clownery and pantaloonery of
these pantomimes have clean passed out of my
head. I believe I no more laughed at them than at
the same age I should have been disposed to laugh
at the grotesque Gothic heads (seeming to me then
replete with devout meaning) that gape and grin
in stone around the inside of the old Round Church
(my church) of the Templars.

I saw these plays in the season 1781-2, when
I was from six to seven years old. After the intervention of six or seven other years (for at school all
play-going was inhibited) I again entered the doors of
a theatre. The old Artaxerxes evening had never
done ringing in my fancy. I expected the same
feelings to come again with the same occasion.
But we differ from ourselves less at sixty and
sixteen, than the latter does from six. In that

interval what had I not lost! At the first period I knew nothing, understood nothing, discriminated nothing. I felt all, loved all, wondered all—

Was nourish'd, I could not tell how—

I had left the temple a devotee, and was returned a rationalist. The same things were there materially; but the emblem, the reference, was gone! The green curtain was no longer a veil, drawn between two worlds, the unfolding of which was to bring back past ages to present a 'royal ghost'—but a certain quantity of green baize, which was to separate the audience for a given time from certain of their fellow-men who were to come forward and pretend those parts. The lights—the orchestra lights—came up a clumsy machinery. The first ring and the second ring was now but a trick of the prompter's bell—which had been, like the note of the cuckoo, a phantom of a voice, no hand seen or guessed at which ministered to its warning. The actors were men and women painted. I thought the fault was in them; but it was in myself, and the alteration which those many centuries—of six short twelvemonths—had wrought in me. Perhaps it was fortunate for me that the play of the evening was but an indifferent comedy, as it gave me time to drop some unreasonable expectations, which might have interfered with the genuine emotions with which I was soon after enabled to enter upon the first appearance to me of Mrs Siddons in *Isabella*. Comparison and retrospection soon yielded to the present attraction of the scene; and the theatre became to me, upon a new stock, the most delightful of recreations.

A COMMENTARY

[HAVING thus followed Lamb through his
dramatic essays, in which he has, with a pleasant
discursiveness, set out various principles that
should regulate acting, the drama, scenic effect, and
the stage generally, I now propose to formulate,
as it were, these principles into a system, reconcil-
ing some apparent contradictions; at the same time
disposing of some theories — fantastic crochets
perhaps—but, in the way of discussion merely,
and not of controversy.]

I.—ON THE TRAGEDIES OF SHAKSPEARE

IN this profound essay Lamb makes a protest
against performing the plays of Shakspeare, on the
ground that it is 'impossible' to *act* them, and that

acting destroys their effect or falsifies the intentions of the poet. On this text he sets out most
of his favourite principles, illustrated, of course,
by some pleasant paradox, or, not a little that is
'fantastical.' Without accepting one rather startling proposition, we find ourselves at the close enriched by many a valuable thought and useful
principle, while the whole throws an abundance of
light on the nature and proper limits of dramatic
entertainment. At the opening he pleasantly urges
that there is something absurd in praising an actor
for interpreting Shakspeare, or in complimenting
him that he has 'a mind congenial to the poet's,'
which assumes, he says, 'that the power of reciting
and interpreting correctly, and that these low
tricks upon the eye and ear, are the same as that
absolute mastery over the heart and soul which a
great dramatist possesses.'   This seems a mis-
apprehension, as such conventional phrases, it is
obvious, mean little.   We might as well assume
that Ruskin when interpreting the beauties of
Michael Angelo, or Raphael, was claiming to be as
great an artist as either.

He then points out, what is better founded, the
danger of identifying the actor with the character;
as, for instance, readers who have frequently
seen the Hamlet of our day, will find their studies
afterwards disturbed by the perpetual dreams of
his image, motions, tones, &c. 'Dearly do we pay,' he
says, for the greater intelligibility of the whole thus
secured, for 'when the novelty is passed, we find to

our cost that instead of realising an idea, we have only materialised *and brought a fine vision to the standard of flesh and blood;'* or to quote what we may consider our text, instead of obtaining 'a fine abstraction,' we have brought the abstraction down, and 'made everything natural.'

This opens up a really interesting question—whether Shakspeare does or does not gain by the interpretation of a great actor. It might be answered that the student at his desk, poring over his loved volume, was lifted too much into the abstract world, and that many a passage, which appears to him perplexing, or at least colourless, becomes perfectly intelligible when uttered with emphasis, and in the real situation. Even in ordinary plays, written by practised stage-wrights, the reader will note passages which seem pointless, or colourless, but, which, to his surprise, when uttered on the boards 'tell' with surprising effect. In a very pleasing essay our leading tragedian has himself dealt with this subject, and has proved convincingly that the actor brings additional light to the text, and supplies a meaning which would otherwise be lost.

There is a little Shakspearian fragment of Lamb's criticism in his 'Table Talk,' which is truly admirable and is an excellent revelation of what such criticism should be. He is speaking of the closing lines of Lear, when the faithful Kent is dimly recognised by the dying king; and here Elia seems effectually to enfeeble his own theory—that

Shakspeare should not be set on the stage—a plea
born of excessive reverence—in a magnificent way.
It might escape the student at his desk, that so
much was intended in these abstract lines. Lear
says, 'Who are you?' and Kent gently tells him;
but without effect, beyond a general—'You are
welcome hither.' The lines, however, should be
read to see the force of Lamb's inspired criticism—
'What a puddle,' he says, 'would a common dramatist have raised here of a reconciliation scene.
The old dying king partially catching at the truth
and immediately lapsing into obliviousness, with
the high-minded carelessness of the other to have
his services appreciated, are among the most
judicious, not to say heart-touching strokes in
Shakspeare.' Now, it is clear that the readers or
students that could pierce to this meaning are
few indeed, but to the thoughtful poetical actor, it
would be suggested by the very situation itself.

In fact, it is certain that a person who first read
over a scene, ever so carefully, and then saw it
acted by capable performers, would be astounded at
all that is evolved, at the wealth of meaning which
a simple line seems to hold, and which is brought
out by movement, and gesture, and acting. The
very grouping suggests.

This presentation, he urges, tells specially
against Shakspeare; as the system reduces everything to 'scolding scenes,' to 'a controversy of
elocution,' or to preachings, &c., so as to impress
what is going on upon the audiences, as an extract

from daily life, and thus destroys what is the
charm of Shakspeare. 'What does not Hamlet
suffer by being dragged forth as a public school-
master to give lectures to the crowd,' whereas nine-
tenths of what he does are 'inner transactions,
communings with himself,' silent meditations,
which cannot be represented by 'a gesticulating
actor, who comes and mouths them out before an
audience.' The love 'dialogues of Romeo and
Juliet,—all the delicacies which are so delightful in
the reading, how are they sullied by being addressed
to an audience—drawling out of the mouth of a
hired actress.' All which commends itself. But the
answer is obvious. First, the objection will apply
to all plays and all acting. Then it may be asked :
Is this, or *must* this be the sole and exclusive mode
of presenting Shakspeare, or does every actor necessarily adopt this form of lecturing the audience—
the scolding matches, &c. ? Lamb is here, therefore,
only urging his grand principle that the material or
realistic system—imported from that of the streets
and interiors of daily life—is fatal to proper dramatic interpretation. There was before his eyes
the 'pavior style'—the pattern of which was set
by Mr Kemble ; and still lingers in the Provinces and on the American stage. The truth
is, since Lamb's day, a complete reformation and
new modes of interpreting Shakspeare have been
applied, and the great dramatic reform introduced by Victor Hugo, of applying the colour
and passions of nature to life, instead of the cold

classic reserve, had not yet passed to England.
And so I fancy as to that 'delightful sense of
freshness' which is felt when we turn to such
plays of Shakspeare which have 'escaped being
performed.' Here the generous enthusiasm of the
writer may have carried him away : for it does
seem that the plays may have 'escaped being performed' on account of their comparative inferiority
—or, if of equal merit, would certainly have been
more appreciated had they been performed. Those
pieces, too, which have been 'spouted,' done to
death, as it were, might appear to have lost their
bloom and freshness ; but I confess the instance
selected, that of 'To be or not to be,' scarcely seems
to support his view. That strange, mysterious,
and perplexing piece of philosophy, every time it
is heard, offers new lights to an intelligent and
sympathetic actor—nay, even with its repetitions
by the same actor, there come revelations and
glimpses of meaning, which make the whole clearer
and more intelligible. In short, .the character
of Hamlet is itself so many sided, and offers such
modes of interpretations—the spiritual, the realistic, the antic, dreamy, revengeful—or may be so
mysteriously compounded of all these, that each
player offers a different view, and is an altogether
different Hamlet. For the time, indeed, it may
be associated with one poetical figure, like the
present cynosure of the public ; but it is curious that
even the Lawrence picture of Kemble in his inky
cloak, moralizing, familiarly enough, on a skull,

suggests even to these who had not seen him, a Hamlet of another order. But the truth is, your true reader of Shakspeare will not allow his ideal to be disturbed by any fleshly embodiment, and will hold all far short of what he desires, while the pure playgoer will be content with what he sees. Nay, even the student playgoer, so far from being disturbed by individual presentments, finds pleasure in comparing and contrasting them, and seems to compound his Hamlet out of many.

To this does not belong that realism as exhibited by Fechter and others which assumes Hamlet to be a gentleman of our day, giving his various speeches quite a colloquial turn, than which nothing can be more opposed to the spirit of Shakspeare. In the common ceremonials of everyday life—such as marriages, receptions at Court—there is imported a certain state dignity, while a familiar tone is out of all keeping. And so in the plays of Shakspeare, everything, diction, era, character, incident, all are removed from this light familiar manner of our life, and should be portrayed in a stately fashion. The very metrical form of the verse require declamation; and, indeed, now-a-days nothing is more offensive to the ear than to hear the fine poetical lines 'gabbled over,' as it may be termed, by some young untrained 'Lord' or courtier, who models his diction on the familiarities of his club. How refreshing, then, when some well trained, 'well graced' performer deigns to declaim his lines, with a musical, melodious rise and fall, and what a meaning, what a new charm is thus imparted !

Next, as for the objection against soliloquies, or communings with oneself, such as those of Hamlet, represented by 'a gesticulating actor, making four hundred people;' or rather, over a thousand — his confidants at once. To do this effectively, it is objected, we must emphasize everything, by 'some trick of eye or tone, and this is the way to represent the shy, negligent, retiring Hamlet.' Yet is it not conceivable that a player might so deliver these soliloquies without any of the 'tricks' alluded to, exactly as though he were unconscious of the presence of the four hundred persons ? So that here again Lamb is evidently thinking of the 'spouters' of his time. Such vulgarity of treatment leads Lamb to suppose that if some inferior dramatist, such as Banks or Lillo, had written 'the process of the story,' leaving out all the divine features of it, giving plenty of passionate dialogue, the acted effect would be much the same as now. The truth is, this very result has been almost brought about on the French stage.

To the French, with the best intention to appreciate and admire Shakspeare, the Bard has ever appeared almost incomprehensible. They lay hold of the melodramatic elements in Hamlet or Macbeth: character and story they can deal with in a sort of rude way, protesting the while against the ludicrous extravagances. While they take this narrow view, they are right enough in reshaping him for their

stage; but the deep philosophy and the many sides
of character familiarized to us by tradition and
constant repetition, are so much Hebrew to them.
The only resource, therefore, for them is the concrete realistic treatment, and Hamlet—in Ducis's
translation, in other versions, as well as in the
absurd opera—becomes a sort of Byron, morbidly
brooding on his wrongs.

'So to see Lear acted,' as an old man tottering
about the stage with a walking stick. 'The Lear
of Shakespeare cannot be acted. The contemptible *machinery by which they mimic the
storm is not more inadequate to mimic the
horrors of the real elements*; while we read
it, we see not Lear, but we are Lear.' And
so with Othello. Nothing, he says, can be more
flattering to the noble parts of our nature than to
find a young lady of rank wedding a real black
moor. . . . 'It is the triumph of virtue
over accidents. She sees Othello in his mind.
But on the stage that colour overpowers everything. Here is something revolting in the courtship. And the reason is that this sense is palpable
to the eyes, whereas there is not enough of belief in
the feeble internal motive.' The true reason, it
seems, for this impression as to Othello's colour,
as well as for the stick and infirmities of Lear,
arises from undue emphasis laid on them. The
idea to be offered is that of a *Moor*. 'The Moor'
must therefore be impressed on the audiences *in
omnibus*, by costumes, colour, &c. The probability

is that any foreign element, such as this was, in a state like Venice, would have a tendency to be assimilated, not to offer such a contrast. Othello would be likely enough to have conformed, in dress and manner, to the country of his adoption.

As to Lear and Macbeth 'with the machinery of the storms and the purposely made hideous old women, who do duty as witches,' the objection is better founded. But this is on account of the undue emphasis laid on them, and the elaborate attempts made to represent the ghostly incidents, which offer the greater failure in proportion to their elaborateness. But while taking these objections, we are helped to a great truth, viz., that this conventional outside mimicry of 'business,' as it is called, destroys the intellectual dramatic effect, and Lamb is really condemning the established system of stage effect of his day.

There are many portions of Shakspeare's dramas dealing with violent storms, pitched battles, 'armies,' and the like, and which bring only dis-illusion, and are opposed to the Shaksperian spirit, but which modern abuse has developed, on the excuse of 'fitting them for the stage.' We tolerate these for the value of the rest of the play. It is most true that the average Lear has been shown as an old man with a white beard, tottering about, and flourishing a crutch stick; but there is no reason why there should not be a Lear of power who should himself fill the stage, and be independent of the vulgar aids reprobated by

Lamb.   One might almost say, indeed, that this
conception of an old man, feeble, with a prodigious
snowy beard, tottering, and 'croaking,' does not
really   awaken   our   best   and   most   effective
sympathies.   There is a suggestion of eccentricity,
for we are apt to associate these as tokens of decay
and insensibility.   It is the sort of sympathy we
feel for the helplessness of a child.   More piteous
far is the old man; who is gallantly suppressing
his infirmities, who is gray and grizzled.   Then as
to his surroundings, the ideal Lear should be set
forth simply without procession or courtiers or
eternal   guards,   gorgeous   palaces,   and   the   rest
which the stage manager holds to be *de rigueur*.
We should appeal to his figure alone, and to
his soul, and trust to it for producing the impression, *indicating* as it were the effect of the
appendages of the scene.   An illustration will show
this.   Suppose that in real life we were sent
for to comfort some aged friend—some nobleman
whose children had behaved ungratefully, who,
after he had stripped himself of all he had, was
cast off, and was now bewailing his own wretched-
ness, and invoking maledictions on them.   Such
a scene would fill all our thoughts.   We would
take little heed of the room, surroundings, what
persons, servants, or furniture, &c., were about
him.   That desolate spectacle of misery would
be enough, and would affect us more.

The   attempting   to   present   supernatural,   or
horror inspiring objects on the stage, Lamb urges

M

must defeat itself on the same reasons. This he pushes so far, to exclude it from the stage altogether, and to admit of nothing save the reader and his volume. But his reasons seem only to apply to existing conventional modes. Thus with those midnight hags, the witches, when we *read* of them, owing to the indistinctness of the operation, we can picture them according to any standard of horror. 'Do we not feel spell bound,' and is not the effect the most serious and appaling that can be imagined. But bring them on the stage, and 'you know them instantly as so many old women that men and children are to laugh at.' '*The sight destroys the faith.*' 'It is the solitary taper and the book that generates a faith in these terrors.' . . . This indeed ever opens most serious difficulties. But the failure seems to have been always caused by attempting *too much* on this side of the supernatural, for which the resources are utterly inadequate. Anything spectral or purely ghostly is associated with the magic lantern or something kindred, and when in Macbeth the ghost was shown in a transparent pillar, by strong light, there was no sense of mystery or horror. The audience felt that they were in the secret and quite understood how it was contrived. Many attempts of the kind have been made to grapple with the supernatural—Wagner's 'steam clouds' imitating the mysterious vapours in which spirits appear, being the latest. But somehow these only suggest steam and nothing more. But the ghost

in Hamlet is a real interesting crux ; and though the
best intellects have been applied to the solution
it has never yet been exhibited in a satisfactory
manner. He is ever too corporeal and *strides* too
much, and we are always prepared for that business
with the truncheon. Here we suffer from the loss
of the old system of lighting—when the stage
seemed to be lit after the fashion an ordinary room
would be lit—*viz.*, by a sufficiency of chandeliers
which left corners and various portions of the room
in natural shadow. Thus it would be that the
ghost would emerge from shadow into the centre
lighted part of the room, and retreat in the same
way. In the present system the room is suddenly
darkened a moment before, so that we know that
the ghost is presently to be expected. All is
darkened, and all is lightened indiscriminately.

So with the inviting of Hamlet to follow him
which is usually done with a stiff gesture, and
waving of the truncheon. But one could fancy the
poor Ghost fluttering away a few steps—inviting
beseechingly, and with imploring face, the other to
follow. A great deal of the usual stiff effect seems
owing to the walk of the Ghost, which is invariably
of a solemn military stride ; the truncheon carried
with arm bent in a constrained fashion. He pro-
menades forwards in a sort of conscious fashion,
and comes to a halt as if at a command. Now, a
ghost might be presumed to be a poor, faltering,
frightened, hesitating creature—he glides about
the world on his sad leave of absence, expecting

summons back to prison. He is not of the earth, but only lent. So instead of marching straight to a person he visits, he might enter hesitating, scared, walking like the rest of the world, but as if he saw no one. Nor should he keep his truncheon at the 'Present,' but down by his side. So in the instance of Banquo's Ghost seen at Macbeth's table. An imaginative man might by an effort reach to the solution which would probably escape our too practical stage managers. He would picture to himself some such scene in our day—the host suddenly become a prey to a delusion; the guests alarmed, scared, whispering, half-rising, this contrasted with the general noise and hilarity existing but a moment before. The figure or ghost, it should be contrived, should be seen *apart*, motionless, and, if possible, not having attracted attention before—just as in 'Vanderdecken,' when the sailors, busy chatting noisily on the sea-shore at early dawn, become conscious of the presence of the Flying Dutchman, who is calmly watching them. This touches an element of the ghostly, discovering that someone has been with us for some time without our being conscious of it. But we can do no more than indicate what it would be the function of an accomplished stage manager to carry out.

So with spirits, fairies, gods, persons with wings, our stage appliances are singularly rude. We cannot, by any possible means, bring ourselves to believe that they belong to any other world. They are simply Mr or Miss ———, wearing

gauze wings fitted to their backs. The principle
to start with is that their divinity lies in their
thought, speech, and action. The dress is but
little; but let us hear Elia:—'Spirits and fairies
cannot be represented; they cannot even be painted;
they can only be believed.' In the next sentence
he passes to the subject of scenery, and in a few
words, hints at this principle, which he expands at
length in the essay we have placed next. 'But
the elaborate and anxious provision of scenery,
which the luxury of the age demands in these
cases, works quite a contrary effect to what is
intended. A parlour, a drawing-room, a library
opening into a garden, a street, does well enough in
a scene. We are content to give it as much credit
as it demands, *or rather we think little about it.* It
is little more than reading at the top of the page—
Scene—a Garden. We do not imagine ourselves
there, but we readily admit the imitations of
familiar objects. But to think by the aid of
painted trees and caverns, which we *know* to be
painted, to transport our minds to Prospero and his
island, and his lonely cell; or by the aid of a fiddle
dexterously thrown in, to make us believe that we
have the supernatural noises,' &c. Admirable
words, and as true as admirable, even if a little
exaggerated, or overlooking the necessities of the
stage.

How true, also, is all that Lamb has laid down
in these illustrations where he speaks of Raphael's
treatment of the subject of the building of the ark,

and of the efforts of painters to pourtray Othello
and Sir John Falstaff, and the scenes in which
they figure. Of the first he says:—'Not to the
nautical preparations with the shipyards at Civita
Vecchia did Raphael look for instructions when he
imagined the building of the vessel that was to be
the conservatory of the wrecks of the species
of drowned mankind. *In the intensity of the
action he ever keeps out of sight the meanness of the
operation.*' Yet this is exactly what the skilful
and enterprising scenic director or *Regisseur* looks
to as his guide and prompting spirit. Some
shipbuilding scene, antique or modern, has to be set
forth. It is made matter of pride, and claims
for praise that 'sketches have been made on
the spot,' that real workmen, tools, and the proper
pattern of operations have been followed with
strictest fidelity. So in the prison scenes, painstaking studies are made of the warders, convicts
going to work in proper dress, &c. The more
minute and abundant these details, the less of the
dramatic, and perhaps the less of illusion there
is present. We are only more brought to real life.
The prisoner and the elements of prison life are
surely shown by exhibiting the mind and passions
under prison influences, the rest should be merely
indicated, to this extent and limit, that nothing
else shall intrude to disturb the sense of prison
life.

A French painter of military subjects has often
issued coloured drawings of French soldiers of the

various arms—the chasseur, private, hussar, &c.
which have an extraordinary dramatic interest and
attraction; yet they are simply and unobtrusively
done, representing the soldier in a common position.
It is only on careful examination that we discover
the secret. With an ordinary journeyman the receipt
is simple enough, and is applied to other groupings
transferred from daily life. A good figure is selected
and drawn. His clothes and uniform are copied
with minutest accuracy. Yet the result has
always a disagreeable and vulgar effect, to the
astonishment perhaps of the painstaking artist
himself, who has only copied nature with a pho-
tographic accuracy. Now, the secret of the accomplished Frenchman lay in this: He had seen and
studied many types, say of his chasseur, and had
thus gathered the general character of this service
—which like every service has a special influence
on its followers. This is not to be obtained by
servile copying of an individual. There is a
peculiar carriage, a careless manner, a dozen little
notes and touches of nature and habit. The single
specimen cannot show all these at the same moment,
or at least they are not to be got from studying
a single man in a studio. And this is the secret of im-
parting to dramatic work an artistic spirit. So with
these pictures of waves, spates, &c., which Hook, Peter
Graham, and others, give with such force and
accuracy. Their work is the result of innumerable
observations, until they have learnt the manner of
waves and their workings—much of which they

have to put on canvas under the influence of a
strong memory and vivid imagination, correcting
and adding by actual observation. Now, a little
reflection will apply all this readily to the impersonation of characters on the stage. One actor will
have before him a spiritual aim, will ignore or
forget mechanical devices, and omit all helps to
expression that are found in ordinary social life.
In this aim he might fail, but the mere intonation
and effort would give his acting a different cast.
Another performer would place his ideal on earth,
and labour at reproducing all that he observed about
him. He would note the gestures of avarice, rage,
humour, &c., would, in short, be as real as he
could. It may be conceived which of these two
systems should be applied to the interpretation of
Shakspeare, either as regards sense, or scene, or
acting. To the latter the spirit of Shakspeare is
certainly repugnant, and yet we have found the
young nobles and courtiers striving to deliver their
lines after the easy model of our daily colloquial
fashion, in the lively intonation of the club-room,
prattling them over, with a view of lightening the
monotony or obliterating the solemn character of
the verse. When it is thought that a Shaksperian
sentence is a quintescence, as it were, and represents the mental situation of the moment, which it
would take many a sentence of our imperfect diction to paraphrase haltingly, it will be felt that it
ought to be declaimed with solemnity and emphasis.

Shakspeare is so intimately connected with the

question of scenery that we are naturally led to consider the limits of this element of dramatic interpretation. Where a question of reform is insisted on, one is likely to go too far, and to seem extravagant: and thus, in such comments one may seem to push theory beyond grounds upon which it is feasible. In a happy sentence at the close of his last essay, Lamb points to what is the usual excess in this matter; 'All these non-essentials,' he says, 'are raised into an importance injurious to the main interest of the play.'

It would not be difficult, after reading Elia, to conceive of an ideal revival of a Shakspearian play, which would be suitable and effective, for bringing out the dramatic meaning and interest, and yet be what is called, 'handsomely mounted.' To show how one very simple and unimportant element is bound up with dramatic sense and instinct, we may point to the later substitution of bright and storied tapestry curtains for the old green baize curtain. Now, this may seem trifling, yet there has been a distinct loss of dramatic interest by the change. When we entered one of the great theatres, *i.e.* 'Old Drury,' where, however, it is still retained, prepared to see a play of strong dramatic interest, there was before us the vast indistinct—a floating sombreness—with something like the indefiniteness of the ocean. There was nothing on which the eye could rest. On the contrary, there was a sense of mystery in that expanse, which occasionally floated and stirred. One felt that behind there was something preparing. It was the grand barrier separating that other world of romance and story from our profane sense. So at the end, when the leading character was stretched out prone, having given up the ghost, it descended with slow moving, successive folds. It seemed to part us forever, from what we had been following. All was done with, when the expanding folds touched the ground—a general blankness!

But now, there is no feeling of this kind—the gaudy fluttering curtains, which we all but see a man pulling together in the midst, are mundane, and belong to our side of the house. There is a frivolous gaiety about them, nothing theatrical— they are pure upholstery, and, as they are drawn away, the feeling left is, that the actors are scarcely separated, and belong to *us*. On such airy nothings does the dramatic sense depend. Again, as to furnishing. The vast modern equipments, with which we are familiar, which crowd the stage at the West End theatres, seem, instead of leading the spectators into ideal realms, to bring the actors and their play within our own domain. It seems to carry, as it were, the well upholstered stall chairs on to the stage. Here, as in other fields of art, furniture and appointments should be idealized. They should be made unobtrusive, and there should be as little of them as possible. The stage, as will be seen later, is intended to represent that clear space, or zone, on which any exciting narrative of life takes place. Of course, if it be made to take the

shape of an enclosed room, with its three out of
four sides shown—this completeness might be insisted on, but the theory is that the stage represents
only that portion of the room which is around the
figures.

The question to be solved, in putting Shakspeare
on the stage, is surely, What is the key to the particular scene—say of the ghostly scenes of Hamlet?
Mystery, surely, and a sense of awe and the supernatural. It would be easy to call up the images of
officers on guard on the platform of an ancient
castle, swept by the sea and keen winds—the cold
night, the blank masses of wall, quite indistinct,
and all shadows. How easily would a picturesque
artist exhibit this on a single 'cloth.' No need of
'building up' towers or drawbridges. There would
be infinitely more horror in this generality. It was
thus that in the Lyceum revival, as originally produced, this sense of mystery—the cold blue of
approaching dawn—was conveyed.

Again, in every Shakspearian play, it has become inevitable that the King, Duke, Noble, Lady,
or any one that holds a court, should have a grand
interior, stately, devoted to their accommodation
with arches, tapestry thrones: while all is preceded
and succeeded, after the inexorable law of the stage
manager, by the 'carpenter's scene.' There is a sad
monotony in all their courtly views of banquets,
groupings, plays, shoutings, trumpets, acclamations,
&c. It reduces the character of the King, Duke,
&c., to a sort of stage conventional type. They

convey nothing courtly, whereas were they less
encumbered they would offer more of individual
character to our minds.   The King in Hamlet
always carries his diadem, even into his closet.
In such pieces, if the King and his retinue
have to enter in state, it would appear that,
for the most intelligent and advanced of stage
managers, there is but one fashion of effectively
impressing this on the audience, namely, by exhibiting them to the best advantage.   The retinue
must   be   introduced,   and   once   introduced, it
must be ranged in some regular order.   Hence
the entrance in military array, and 'forming up'
so as to make a symetrical group.   No ingenuity,
it will be said, can get rid of this disposition   The
larger and more richly dressed the 'Court,' the
more effective the result.   Hence the disparaging
association in the spectator's mind of the 'super.'
And so familiar is every audience with the mechan-
ism and apparatus, that it may be affirmed safely,
that no delusion of awe or majesty is left, but
we invariably think of these dummy personages
as what they really are, 'show men,' engaged at a
shilling or two.   It will be reasonably asked, what
should your reformer do?   The answer would not
be difficult, if these principles were borne in mind,
namely, to *indicate* rather than present the idea of
an abundant attendance, and this should be like
the indistinct figures on a tapestry.   Nature, life,
should be taken as a guide, to a certain extent.   When
a great personage holds an interview of state, his re-

tinue of two or three persons stand afar off in review, as it were, not formally drawn up, but seeming careless. The number of figures should be regulated as in real life, by the proportion of space on the stage, for these great crowds are not huddled together within limited area, but by a sort of instinct a group finds itself with plenty of space about it. It should be so with the furniture, if it be used. How absurd it seems to see an exciting episode carried on in a richly appointed drawing room, the figures having scarcely room to turn!

From the last days of Kemble, the public has been delighted with a service of Shakspearian Revivals, magnificent shows, which it was assumed, *sans dire*, were effective in proportion to their magnificence for the illustration of the Bard. This system has been pursued down to the late superb Lyceum Revivals, which have eclipsed all that has gone before. Yet it almost seems as though Shakspeare hardly gained by this process. It makes all too detailed, while the Bard intended all to be general. It brings us nearer to earth, while he wafted us higher into the spiritual world. These vistas of streets, gorgeous halls, long-drawn processions, splendid robes, over-weight the particular episodes where they are introduced, destroy their proportion to the real dramatic interest. The author only intended such as an allusion *en passant*. It is always forgotten too, that the stage and its surroundings is really only proportioned to the

action of a few figures. The actor himself forms
a standing scale by which the audience must
measure everything, and to which the scenery ought
to be proportioned. And though illusion is brought
to aid by means of painting, and distance and sky
may be magnified, still the *ground* is a fixed
quantity.   The notion, therefore, of crowding
masses of figures, processions, furniture, buildings,
&c., into this contracted area causes a sort of scenic
congestion. It really supplies the idea of narrowness
and poverty, instead of grandeur and magnificence.

Again, there must be an excuse for display, and
shifts are found to make crowds defile, so as to show
their numbers. In Much Ado About Nothing, where,
in the tomb scene, a number of persons with flaming
torches enter as usual and fill the stage, standing
very much in front close to the footlights, owing to
'the cloth' being far forward, the effect is imposing
and even grand, but no sense of imagination can
make one suppose that we are transported to a
mysterious mausoleum.   It was a number of men
bearing lights on a raised platform. Not long ago,
on the opening of 'Bell's Theatre,' I came on one of
Stothard's (or one of his school) exquisite little
vignettes of the same scene.   There were two or
three figures in the centre—the solitary mystery of
the tomb around, the reviving hero, an air of tenderness and grace, and one felt that such treatment as
his was simple and tranquil, and indeed the whole
gains by leaving it to the imagination to suggest
the rest.

Take again the scene of Ophelia's burial. The usual way by which, it is believed, effect is given to Shakspeare's directions, is to develop the situations by funeral procession, music, church cloisters, grave-yard, &c. These elements seem to lessen the effect of the leading figure. The eye wanders over a crowd of objects, and inanimate, amid which Hamlet is lost. An indistinct gloomy back-ground of trees, solitary, and with that air of loneliness which is seen in many a graveyard— and nothing else—this would 'throw out' the figure; nor would we have the shovelling out of the actual clay, the heaps of bones, &c., for one knows that is only an open 'trap' made in the boards, betrayed by the very sound. So with the procession, with its monks, &c. There is the idea too, of 'the maimed rites,' which suggests something hurried, secret, and curtailed. Hence, there should be no music or other solemnities. What if two or three shadowy figures appeared among the trees, bearing the body thus consigned to the earth hastily: the King and Queen entering in their characters of person-ages in the drama, but without the conventional train; and this suggest again that this *literalness*, accounting for the various stages, &c., is foreign to the *abstract* of the stage. It is enough that the King and Queen were found there. It is a super-fluous assumption that they must have come at the tail of a long train. All that we are entitled to deduce from the situation, is that a beautiful girl is interred, in a hurried fashion, under a cloud as it were.

The question of what may be called Archiac Revival offers much interesting speculation. Here there must surely be a *limit*. Minute reproduction of antique costume seems to be mere pedantry, and is lost on an audience, which is either ignorant or indifferent. The rich and gorgeous dresses now in vogue, and fashioned out of costly 'plushes' copied from the old portraits of Moroni and Pordenone, seem to overpower the features and (fantastic as the thought may be) actually take off from the weight of the utterance, for the attention is drawn away, and the eye is attracted rather than the ear.

It will help us in these interesting speculations, if we consider for a moment one magnificent and ambitious scene which was the glory of the revived Much Ado About Nothing. This splendid effort, which reflected the taste and daring of Mr Irving, has never been surpassed on any stage, has given unalloyed pleasure, and excited boundless admiration. But 'we are now considering it as an illustration, whether the text of Shakspeare gains or loses by such additions. The scene, it will be remembered, portrayed a grand cathedral interior with high altar, choir gates, arching roof, pillars and lamps, processions, acolytes, censers, friars, &c., &c., and here was the heroine publicly rejected by her suitor, in presence of a brilliant wedding party of gaily dressed courtiers. Consulting the author himself we find the scene indeed to be 'the Church,' but scarcely such a church as the latest interpretation of our modern stage would warrant. We find the marriage about to take place, the guests assembled, the interruption — followed by the playful rallyings of Benedict, and his promise to Beatrice, which again is succeeded by the glimpse of the humours of the watch, and Dogberry's protest against being 'written down an ass'—all before the high altar, where the lamps of the sanctuary are burning.

The stage manager will hold that the situation is intractable, and so much the worse for Shakspeare, who must be fashioned into some reasonable shape. And yet, taking the larger abstract view, this is only the indifference or forgetfulness of trivial details, which a serious crisis really induces; we find that Shakspeare is here harmonious enough, and could be treated after his own spirit with due stage effect. Suppose it were related of an evening, at a fashionable London dinner, how that morning at St George's, Hanover Square, there had been a scandal—the bride waiting at the altar, the bridegroom had refused to go on, on the ground of some surprising discovery made that very morning, with fainting, &c.; and after sympathy or reprobation duly expressed, it might be added how it was likely to bring about another marriage, for that a certain confirmed and mercenary bachelor had been seen comforting Miss——, one of the bridesmaids. Now no listener would suppose that all this took

N

place before the altar, or inquire where. The dramatic connection or sequence was sufficient. It grew out of the first transaction. It might have been on the steps of the church, while waiting for the carriages or in the vestry. In short, this finding locality or scenes for every incident—this 'localising with all the accuracy of ocular admeasurement,' as Lamb put it, is out of keeping. To give a separate scene to each of the three incidents would unduly magnify the two last, which are mere *obiter dicta* as compared with the first.

How then is it all to be expressed? Not without difficulty certainly, but the task is made easy, or easier, by following the Shakspeare spirit. In foreign countries the church was not a place for service on Sundays, but a sort of public place open all day; a place of tryst and passage, with its dependancies and cloisters, and passages and vestibules, and colonades. A marriage rarely takes place at the high altar, but at some side altar or little chapel, into which, it may be, one passing along the arcade can look in and see what is going on. This general idea of 'the church' is sufficient, and inconsistent with that fixing of the characters, hard and fast, before the high altar. All that Shakspeare conveyed was that the incident took place under the roof of the church, or 'at the church.' He so disdainéd to be specific, that his Act is without naming any place or scene at all.

The conspicuousness, importance, and weight of leading characters, as in Hamlet, is seriously

lessened by being surrounded with gaudily illuminated ' sets ' full of glittering details. The eye is
distracted, the character itself does not command
our exclusive attention. It seems part of the
gaudiness about him. So with the innumerable
figures, arrayed in glittering fabrics, that crowd
the stage; which by the smallness of the space, are
crowded and grouped about him in a way it would
not be in real life. So with the play of Romeo and
Juliet treated *realistically*, the crowd and fighting
in the streets, Mercutio's abrupt speech about Queen
Mab, the tangible marriage by the Friar, the
emphasizing of the ' faction fighting,' all which
drag down and overpower the idyllic character
of the piece. In the latest ' mounting ' of the
play, the ' faction fighting,' is given great promin-
ance, and we have enormous crowds of ' Supers,'
doing battle before us. Yet this was only indicated
by the author, and the intelligence of the audience
can supply such incidents sufficiently, as it is all
conveyed in the relation of Romeo to the Capulets.
One feels at the close of this street conflict that it
is out of proportion. It might actually be a
revolution, whereas it was merely a scuffle. The
distinct incidents of the ' biting of the thumb,'
&c., are swallowed up in the noise and confusion of
the battle, and in the recent revival by Miss Anderson, there was a tremendous struggle maintained
for many minutes, men wrestling, and contorted,
falling, &c.—the audiences looking on at all the
elements of individual defeat and victory. All

that the poet intended was to show that there
was a state of hostility between the factions. It
was to be lightly touched and let pass; with so
Homeric a struggle, it dwarfed the rest of the
act. We expected serious consequences to result,
and yet nothing followed.

At the opening of the play Romeo meets Juliet at
the fête given by her father, and we are shown the
whole stage crowded with dancers, amid which the
leading characters are quite lost. Here Juliet is
kissed by her new lover whom she has now seen
for the first time, and whose name even she does
not know. To enable this to take place with some
show of probability the dancers have to disperse.
Now, this whole treatment of the situation is
conceived according to modern rules, and certainly
not in a Shakspearian spirit. This sudden and
rapturous devotion is sacred to retirement and
retreat. It is assumed that this passion, though
instantaneous, has lasted long. It is not to be
disturbed by crowded figures and dancers. These
should be far off—the music at a distance. The
real music should be in the enchanting cadences
of the lovers, and there should be nothing vulgar,
as though it were a pause in some modern ball.

There was an admirable criticism passed to this
play, which is founded on the best and truest
principles that must commend themselves to all.
The poetry is in the substance, as well as in the
form of the play. Take that away—represent

it prosaically and realistically—and it is debased
and corrupted.

'Played in this matter-of-fact modern fashion, the
circumstance which lies beneath all the delicate
poetry is forced upon us with jarring obtrusiveness.
A girl has fallen in love at first sight with the
'goodly outside' of a man with whom she has
scarcely exchanged a dozen sentences. Juliet
has seen her lover but once; she knows nothing of
him but that he is one forbidden by prudence
and family ties; yet is she ready to sacrifice
friends, safety, kindred, everything but honour,
that the overmastering impulse of the passion
inspired by Romeo's good looks may be gratified.
*If the scene is acted prosaically, that aspect of
the matter comes out with unnecessary force.*
Shakspeare has done his part to prevent it by
fashioning a thousand poetical images, and by
throwing the whole conversation into a form
which, as Lord Lytton observes, is purely lyrical.
It is for the stage Romeo and Juliet to carry
out his conception by rendering it with a manner
and tone as far removed from realism as possible.
To be merely light and pleasant in this scene is
to give it a totally wrong significance.

'The defects of the representation struck me very
forcibly in the parting-scene of the third act.
Play *that* scene realistically and prosaically, and
the result is, in the first place, something that is
not Shakspeare's 'Romeo and Juliet;' in the second,
something that is no fit subject for the theatre at

all. No modern dramatist could venture to give
us such a scene ; it would be hissed off the stage of
the Palais Royal. In this, as in the whole play,
there is a mingling of refined and beautiful ideality
with that which is purely sensuous. In Miss
Anderson's rendering of the passage it does seem
to me that this latter element is given undue and
undesirable prominence. Her gestures, her dress,
her display of the physical manifestations of
passion, all emphasize the peculiar situation in
which the wedded lovers are placed ; and, as if to
leave us no doubt on this point, the scenic artist
kindly allows us to behold the nuptial couch in a
conspicuous corner of the stage. I might attempt
to show how the same striving after realism has
gone far to mar the conscientious and careful
labours of stage manager and decorator. No doubt
the scenes and sets may be archæologically perfect ;
possibly they are much more like mediæval Verona
than anything we have had on the stage before.
But do they heighten the effect of the play ? For
my part, I cannot think they do. After all, Shakspeare probably was not thinking of mediæval
Verona and historical accuracy when he wrote
' Romeo and Juliet.' The stage directions tell us
that the scene is laid in Italy ; but its real *locale* is
the land of love and fancy, wheresoever that may
be.' All this is founded on the best part of Lamb's
theory as to the unsuitability of Shakspeare's plays
for representation, or, rather, as we have seen, for
this debased form of representation.

THUS far we have been led to the conclusion that the entertainment of the stage is purely intellectual and emotional, and that the aids of mechanical appliances, being material or imitative, instead of assisting, as is vulgarly assumed to be the case, only diminish the illusion of the entertainment. This applies both to scenery and to acting, and indeed, it might fairly be worked out in most departments of the art, where simple imitation is the lowest form of art. It will be easy, as it is an agreeable task, to illustrate the sound principle here laid down, though much of the charm is owing to Elia's own inimitable style. A passage in his Shakspeare essay seems to embody the whole, or at least strikes the key-note. 'This is the inevitable consequence of imitating everything to make all things natural, whereas, the reading of a fine tragedy is a fine abstraction. It presents to the fancy just so much of external appearances as to make us feel that we are among flesh and blood, while by far the greater and better part of our imagination is employed upon the thoughts and internal machinery of the character. But in acting—scenery, dress, the most contemptible things call upon us to pronounce upon this naturalness.' This principle, though strictly applied to the distinction between reading a play and seeing it acted, is at the root of all later attempts at realism, and enforces the truth that the object of all that comes on the stage, whether drama, actor, or scene, ought to be to present ' *a fine abstraction*,' and not by imitating all things, ' make everything natural.'

In this essay, which is most intimately connected with the stage, he speaks of what may be called the literal or 'earthy' effect, which certain painters, with excellent intentions, produce when treating ideal subjects. This arises from ' copying what is before us.' He takes Martin's great picture ' Belshazzar's Feast,' as an illustration, which from its vast architectural properties and crowds of figures was considered in his day sublime. 'There we see the huddle, the flutter, the bustle, the escape, the alarm at the apparition—all duly exhibited by the well-dressed lords and ladies in the Hall of' Belus.' The stage manager grouping his performers

in Sardanapalus' Court might well take such for
his model, and produce a much admired effect; the
leading actors might work, as it is called, on the
same lines—attitudes of horror, hands uplifted,
faces turned away and shrouded. Yet as Lamb
explains there is ' higher imagination' in the reading than this. 'Is this vulgar fright,' he asks,
'such as we have witnessed at a theatre on a slight
alarm of fire, an adequate exponent of a supernatural terror ? Human fear is ever disturbing,
restless, and bent on escape; the divine fear is
bound down, effortless, passive—The crowd would
have remained *stupor-fixed.*' Then he lays down
this canon, which is of immense value, and, it seems to
me, should regulate all stage presentation, whether
of scenery or speech. 'Not all that is optically
possible to be seen, is to be shown in every picture.'
Thus, in a vast and gorgeous painting, such as that
of the ' Marriage of Canæ,' crowded with costumes
and jewels—there is no dramatic moment—and
every object seems to have a claim to attention. We
pass from one object to the other, and survey each
as one might walk round the splendidly set out
table. But in a day of terrors the eye should see
only in masses and indistinction. Not only female
attire and jewellery exposed to the critical eye of
fashion, have no business in this great subject—
there was no leisure for them. The great masters
worked by ' not showing the true appearances ; that
is, not all that was to be seen at any given moment
by any indifferent eye, but only what the eye might

be supposed to see in the doing or supposing of some portentous action.' So at the moment of the destroying of Pompeii, there might of course be seen the houses tottering, the men and women standing, the thousand and one incidents and attitudes of consternation. 'But what eye saw them at that eclipsing moment, which reduces confusion to a kind of unity, where sight and hearing are a kind of feeling only.' Admirable most significant language! and of infinite force in the question of the stage. There all such accessories, for the same reason, should be indicated, faintly, as it were, and only sufficiently enough for the business of the moment or situation. The effect should operate negatively. Connected with this, is the strange delusion that so-called realism must be dramatic, and that the exact transference of material objects, or the nice simulation of objects and movement belonging to social life is more than sufficient to satisfy our taste. It is thus that buildings, furniture, omnibuses, and cabs are transferred to the stage; but with a result the very opposite of what was so confidently expected. These things, seen every day, after the first surprise, leave no feeling of interest or pleasure. We go to the play to see what we cannot find elsewhere. If it be for incident, it is for that class of incident that so rarely occurs to ourselves or others, that we cannot hope to be so likely to experience it; or for those refinements of emotion high above the somewhat vulgar level of ordinary life. We go to the stage to escape from

life, to find something that is in a manner spiritual;
to be taught the elegant secrets of philosophy. Such
a feeling, for instance, we experience in reading
poetry, when we come on the lines so often quoted—

'The little rift within the lute
That makes the music mute.'—

which in hard prose would amount to the declara-
tion that slight bickering extinguishes all love
and regard. As Lamb himself puts it, 'We have
been spoiled with a tyrant more pernicious to our
pleasures, the exclusive and all-devouring drama
of common life, where, instead of the fictitious, half-
believed personages of the stage, we recognise
ourselves, our brothers, aunts, kinsfolks, allies,
partners, enemies, the same as in life. We carry
our fireside concerns to the theatre with us. We do
not go thither to escape from the pressure of reality,
so much as to confirm our experience of it.'
Admirable and acute criticism, exactly descriptive,
it will be admitted of that oppressive and tedious
tyranny, under which we have so long groaned.
Who has not felt this when submitting to
the ordeal of the average drama, where though
an exciting story has been set out, the men and
women seem to have stepped from the street to the
stage?

All this, indeed, is but the common principle
of the other arts—painting, poetry, music, sculpture.
The ordinary painter copies some incident, vividly
and exactly it may be, but the result is simply

an *imitation* of reality.   The true artist, while
imitating, to a certain extent, has thought only
of the poetry or suggestiveness of his subject, and
appeals to much more.   This might be illustrated
by the principles of true portrait painting, where
the vulgar ideal is of a perfect likeness, copied
literally, as if by photograph.   'It must be like,'
will be the criticism, if the shape, colour, &c.,
be accurately followed.   This question was happily
raised in a late trial, and did something to
enlighten the ignorant, though there was some
obscurity as to that 'investing with artistic merit.'
A simple cast from the human face might seem
the most realistic likeness or copy of all, and yet be
no portrait.   For the true artist will seek even
in the plainest and most prosaic alderman's face for
some intellectual light, some poetry of rude sense
and quick intelligence, some turn of shrewdness
which will interest;   and he will look on the accurate delineation of the features, though necessary,
as something secondary—a mechanical function.
This illustrates forcibly the principle which should
direct the transference of real life and real things—
the crowd idly supposing that the accurate copying
of the bold manners of social life is sufficient
to excite the dramatic sense.   It was thus assumed
that the 'Robertsonian Comedy' with its transcript
of the fade and colourless utterances of dandies and
girls, the making of tea, &c., were dramatic elements just as much as the introduction of real fire;
things, as I have said, which are only a *continuance*

of the real life outside, and cause no sense of change or novelty. Of course, the insipidity of dandy life is a subject for comedy, but the art is shown not in simple transference of inane talk, but in the piercing to the essence of the folly and selecting what is truly significant of the mental formation of the person.

And what a fund of meditation in that passage about the Dryad, ' when an artist is called to paint "on demand" a Dryad, a naked figure, and furnished about with oaks, &c.—or it might be a Naiad, when he surrounds the same figure with fountains and falls of pellucid water!' Yet, how well he shows how the presumption is that influences of the surroundings should be expressed by the figure itself. And this is exactly what should operate on the stage, where the character should be equally independent of the scenery. Mr Ruskin in an exquisite passage has expressed the same idea. He describes himself, in presence of a striking scene in the Jura, as making the experiment with a view of arriving at the sources of its impressiveness, of imagining it for a moment a scene in some aboriginal forest of the New Continent. He says he well recalls the sudden chill and blankness which came over him. ' The flowers lost their light; the hills became desolate ; a heaviness in the boughs of the darkened forest, showed how much of the former had been dependent on a life which was not theirs. Those ever-springing flowers

had been dyed by the deep colours of human endurance, valour, and virtue.'

The progress of science has curiously aided
the scenic movement, for without the existence of
the lime-light, the glittering clothes, the armour,
the brilliant hues of the scene, could never have
displayed their sheen to advantage. The rich plush
stuffs now manufactured in profusion, and the
'silver armour'—a modern discovery—have also
contributed to the show. Yet the thought often
suggests itself—Does the brilliant view of a street
in Venice, bathed in a flood of a gaudy glaring
light, really resemble anything in the outside
world; or have not training and habit made us
accept these conventional forms in despite of
reason? Certain it is that this unnatural and
Plutonian atmosphere with its adjuncts must, of
necessity, overwhelm the actors and the acting. It
attracts the chief part of the spectators' attention,
and makes the actors appear inferior. Under the
older dispensations of the last century, four
chandeliers, suspended over their heads, supplied
the needful light, and the scenery was a simple
painted screen behind, in low colouring, and but
faintly illuminated. Hence, we can see how much
the force, the impression, of the figures was inten-
sified. They, and all they said, at once rivetted
attention. There was nothing to look at, or attend
to but the players.

Again, modern scenery is now constructed on
the 'building-up' principle. Great houses and

other buildings, streets, &c., are all fashioned in
their actual form, and drawn on the stage by
numbers of men, and, as one scene does for an act,
there must be sufficient time to rear these edifices.
The ' cloth ' is but rarely used, perhaps because it
looks poor and ridiculous in company with so much
solid matter.   But is not this ' building-up ' system
really opposed to the illusion of the stage ?   The
stage is but a small area, under the most favourable
conditions, reaching to same forty or fifty feet in
width, by, say, a hundred feet in depth.   In this
contracted   space,   the   scene-builder   proposes   to
exhibit a market-place, for instance, in an Italian
city.   Houses, fountain, flights of stairs, streets—
—all are brought together in one view.   In real
life, only a fragment of these things could be seen
at once from the same point of view.   Possibly it
may be urged that from the distance at which the
spectator is seated, the eye would take in all the
objects named.   But, then, they would be far
smaller and more indistinct, according to the rules
of perspective.   The living figures supply the scale
of proportion.   As it is, the arrangement is all at
fault.   For these ' built up ' structures are on a
miniature scale, the tallest house being only some
two or three times the height of the performer.   It
is like the apparition of a human face in a puppet
show.   The whole is, in short, an attempt to com-
bine the conditions of reality with the conditions
of illusion.
    The   statement   of   a   few   simple   principles—

conceded by all—will help us to a clear understanding of the matter. It will be found that
scenic effect depends on the same principle as
dramatic effect. In both it is found, not in details,
but in the essence of a number of details, as the
untrained dramatist soon finds out to his astonishment. In real life when a genuine or exciting
dramatic situation occurs, it is surely not while
richly-dressed people are symmetrically grouped
around, nor in the exact centre of palatial apart-
ments, nor at the moment that a procession is
passing, nor with magnificent furniture appointments and decorations specially arranged. These
things rarely enter into the situation. A battle is
a grand complex panorama to the mind; but the
real battle, to those who have witnessed it, is but a
few men grouped near, and a cloud of smoke. The
death of Lord Chatham, as painted by Copley,
showing the House of Lords in all its extent,
and all the peers in a vast crowd gathered round,
is a good memorial. But those who witnessed the
dramatic moment saw nothing of this, or saw it
all faintly. For them there was only the dying
orator and his agonies, and perhaps the one or
two who supported him and who entered into
the action.

The simple answer to the question, ' What is
" *the scene* " ? ' will help to clear up the matter more
effectually. The ' Scene ' has, indeed, come to have
a limited technical meaning, as applied to the whole
surroundings of the action, either painted or ' built

up.' But it has a more abstract or general sense by which it seems to imply the dramatic moment of interest arising out of a situation, where two personages, for example, are engaged in a room, either conversing or arranging a conspiracy, or busy with some other dramatic purpose. If they are interrupted by a third, he '*enters on the scene*,' and adds a fresh dramatic element. But, by our present very material scenic laws, this process is always carried out with a *literal* exactness. From the moment of the actor's appearance at the entrance, his progress must be according to the strict conditions of real life ; there must be a door for him to open and close, and from the door he must be followed across the real carpet till he joins the party in the centre. Yet surely in the case of a dramatic incident in real life these things are not thought of, noticed, or remembered. The late Lord Derby expressed the idea happily enough when he said ' he never knew whether it was John or Thomas that answered the bell.' For him it was simply the servant—or indeed the message he carried. A man who has been present at an exciting scene in some room, does not recall whether or how the door was opened, or how the person entered. All he remembers is that the person came and joined the party. He recollects that all were standing in the *centre* part of a great room, with a general notion of furniture, &c., in the background, which made no particular impression on him. But what took place within the zone that

o

held the figures is vividly before him. So, when we read 'Scene—a Street,' it is not meant that a whole street should be displayed to convey to our greedy senses that something took place in the street. In real life, a person who has witnessed some dramatic episode 'in the street,' bears away with him a kind of abstract notion of 'street,' a corner, with a house or two as background. This generally is all that dramatic action asks for; more interferes with its effects, and is surplusage. Hence, the merit of what was called 'old stock scenery,' when there was one general view of 'a street' used in almost every play, a palace interior, a church, a cottage, which scenery did service in every drama. Of course there would be an absurdity in using an English street scene for an Italian play; but there is no doubt the scenery could be much more generalized than it is, and particular scenes could be used for many plays.

And this principle applies particularly to the fashionable practice, before alluded to, of loading the stage with heavy furniture and 'built up' scenes—obstructions, as they might well be called. For the theory of the stage, or 'the scene,' it must be repeated, is that it is a segment or fragment of the ground on which human figures move, and which should be clear and unencumbered. In real life, where anything dramatic occurs, one is conscious of this clear space, and when we recall it, the furniture, &c., seems to recede into indis-

tinctness. ' The Stage ' offers this ideal space,
and the necessary encumbering objects belonging
to the enclosing screens should be painted on the
canvas. With this, too, is connected the problem
of the position of the audience or spectator. Is he
looking on, Asmodeus-like, from afar off, the wall
of the room being removed to allow him to see
what is going on ; or is that wall *behind* him—
is he supposed to be in the room, and, though
virtually at a distance, presumed to be close to the
performer ? The adoption of the first theory really
seems to have led to all the cumbrous abuses in
the matter of scenery. For the opening, which
is covered by the curtain, thus becomes a sort of
' peep-show ' ; everything, as we have shown, must
be compressed and dwarfed so as to give a complete
view—a complete cathedral interior, drawing-room,
market-place, square, street, interior of a cottage,
all must be fitted to the one Procrustean standard,
while, oddest of all, the area of the cottage interior
is equal to the area of the interior of the Italian
market-place.

Taking our original principle as the basis of
all scenic effect, we shall see at once how it dis-
poses of the ingenious but inconclusive effects,
which the ingenuity of modern artists have devised,
such as the stage divided, by a partition, into two
or even four chambers, in each of which we see a
different action going on. Nothing could be more
rude, and ridiculous even, than the partition thus
set, whose bare edge is thrust outward to the

audience, and from which the wall has been, as it were, torn away. Even accepting this as fiction, we see the characters come forward far beyond the boundary, so that we always feel that they have simply to glance, as it were, round the corner, and a single step would land them in their neighbours' room! To be logically accurate, the wall should come down to the very orchestra. But it is an absurd shift, and contradictory of accepted stage illusion. In truth our ideal conception of the stage is that of successive actions in a fixed place; that spot of ground on which the action takes place is typical, and the abstract of *every* place and situation, and unchangeable. These duplicate scenes, therefore, are arbitrary and unmeaning, and it will be found that, even in dramatic construction, they give no help, and are mere surplusage; as in the instance in the 'Solicitor's Office,' with the ante-room, and where the visitor is seen waiting while a murder takes place in the inner room. Beyond tickling the eye, there is nothing gained by this arrangement which could not be gained, with more effect too, by the old simple way.

Another theory really obtained till so lately as thirty years ago, when the stage represented not a complete interior or a complete area of any kind, but merely a segment. When there was a 'Flat' exhibited, with 'side scenes' to mark the exits and entrances, there was simply a background for the performers. They were not enclosed, and for persons in the pit and stalls, the background was there, just as it was for the actors. They were only further removed. This system of flats, or painted cloths, may be considered the truly ' scenic ' one. By it, it is given to the painter to produce the effects with which the stage mechanic and 'builder up' finds it impossible to grapple. The painter, by the arts of perspective and effects of colour, can supply enormous distance, heights as enormous, and subdue all to a proper proportion. More remarkable, however, is the effect of largeness and dignity in the action of the personages, which the use of flats and side-scenes supplies. Take the case of a 'Chamber in a Palace.' It is now usually presented as a sort of deep box with the side towards the audience removed. The flanking walls always give the idea of contraction and restraint. But·under the old system it seemed to stretch away to the right and left behind the scenes. We were only looking at a portion of the great chamber, the portion with which we were directly concerned, because the characters were there. Under this system too, the character entered and 'came on the scene,' not through a door, but from behind a side-scene, thus carrying out the idea that we see him only in his passage to join the characters. He had entered by the door, which might be somewhere behind the scenes. As we have seen, it did not matter, for dramatic purposes, how or when he entered ; all that we were concerned with was the zone, as I have called it, of dramatic interest, in the centre of the chamber, and his passage to it. This and all that flows from it, tends to a largeness and dignity in the dramatic action. In this shape, of course, it is merely a rude principle, but with study and development it would be the foundation of a wonderful reform and would lead to the heightening of genuine dramatic effect. Again, the system of *intense* lighting has operated seriously to the enfeebling or overpowering of dramatic effect. Now the whole stage is bathed and suffused in light from above and below. This has been prompted by the necessity of lighting-up all the accessories of remoter portions of 'the show.' Thus what is more to the front receives an undue portion of the light. This general suffusion, besides being quite false to nature, robs the figures of proper contrast, for even in the case of intense sunlight in the open air, there is abundance of shadows, which are not found on the stage. The older system in the pre-Garrick days was infinitely better, but then it was not intended to illuminate the materials, objects, and decorations. The four heavy chandeliers that hung down half-way over the heads of the actors lit up just the zone in which they stood.

In other directions, too, we see a great mistake, when it is attempted by a literal representation, on a limited area, to convey the presentment of what is real. This is physically impossible, and the failure is in proportion to the ambition of the attempt. Take the instance of 'an army,' or a

procession, or some retinue. The mode now is to
enlist a vast number of supers, arm and drill them,
and then marshal them across the stage. By stage
law they take the one course, defiling down to the
foot-lights, passing across, and turning transversely
up to the back, where they spread out their ranks.
This is assumed to be most effective, but, in truth,
the effect only shows the poverty of the device;
for how can some fifty, or even a hundred men,
squeezed into a space forty or fifty feet square,
convey the idea of an army? Formerly half-a-
dozen 'soldiers' did for the purpose, but this
ridiculous force was no more absurd as representing
'an army' than the hundred men. At this moment
such displays have become so conventional and
familiar that they no longer impress. In real life,
when a general comes to visit a potentate, he does
not enter at the head of his 'army' and defile
round the room in such a style. So with battles
on the stage, which somehow never appear natural,
and generally verge on the ludicrous, however
well done.

It will be easily seen how the present system
has grown into a vice which is impoverishing the
stage, to say nothing of an impoverishment yet
more literal. To the old system of 'cloth' and side-
scene should, of course, be applied all the resources
of art, and great improvement might be made on
the old and rude methods. The properties could
be brought out with a startling vividness. I
have seen attempts in this direction which for

effect were indistinguishable from the most elaborately 'built up' efforts. One single result proves
that the existing system is wrong, since it is
impossible to change the scene once set in its place.
The true ideal of a theatre is a succession of plays;
with the 'cloth' system, the trouble of changing
scene and scenery counts as nothing. But the intelligence of the reader will deduce innumerable
other blessings and advantages certain to flow
when this devouring ogre has been destroyed.

A few 'canons,' based on the principles we have
been considering, will be useful as a summary:—

1. The background, surroundings, &c., of a dramatic incident should be as unimportant or sub-
sidary on the stage as they are always in real life.

2. The less the importance given to scenery, the
more that of the figure increases.

3. The abundance of light now shed upon the
scene diminishes the relief of the figures, whereas
the comparative shade, or indistinctness of the
background, throws out the figures. The colouring
should be low in tone.

4. The object of scenery is negative rather than
positive — the exclusion of the homely outside
world and its details, with the creation of an
illusive world ; instead of which the aim now
appears to be to introduce the outside world and
all its details, and join the stage to real life.

5. As dramatic character, diction, &c., is all
general, so the same principle should be, as far as
possible, applied to scenery. .

6. The scene is the immediate segment of locality where the incident occurs; not a complete representation of the room, street, courtyard, &c.

7. The relative proportion of surrounding objects to the figures, as well as the sense of distance, can only be conveyed by painting. Painting conveys the illusion of relief far more effectively than material imitation.

8. The sense of dramatic *interest* and excitement is kindled more powerfully when left to the un-aided exertion of the performers; shows, vast groupings, elaborate 'built-up' effects, more or less enfeeble the dramatic effect.

Having obtained *these principles* to guide us, we enter more minutely on the consideration of the limits by which scenery should be bounded, for it must be admitted that, as Burke said of the power of the Crown, 'it has increased, is increasing, and ought to be diminished.'.

Minutely accurate details of scenery, based on archæological research, instead of aiding, seem to enfeeble illusion. In the earlier times—so late, indeed, as the beginning of this present century—'A Street'—'Interior of ———'s House '—'A Forest'—was the mode of description, and a set of 'general' scenes were used for nearly all plays. Of course there was the objection that an English street would not serve for an Italian or a French one. But, on the other hand, the detailed accurate reproduction brings enormous difficulties. If it be an Italian street, then it must be a street of the particular town, and the particular town at the particular era, which it would be hard to guarantee. On the other hand, keeping in view the principles we have hinted at, such a segment as one might see who was looking on, we might conceive the idea being conveyed of 'buildings'—a background with an open causeway or road, which would be common to all cities. In the Ammergau play, there was some such fixed scene which seemed to be half in the open air, and half under cover. We might at least be satisfied with a set of 'stock' scenes—some 'generally' Italian, or French, or English, as the case might be. And if carefully and handsomely done, the impressions left on the mind would be much the same as that left by the late sumptuous revivals. Any one now recalling Othello, the Merchant of Venice, Romeo and Juliet, Much Ado, Twelfth Night, or Hamlet, would find it a little difficult to distinguish between the scenery and dresses of each, and would own that much of the scenery and dress would have served indifferently for all.

One of the inconveniences of what is called the 'carpenter's scene,' is, that it hinders illusion, and makes : the action that takes place during its term, of a make-shift and unimportant character. As in the scene in Hamlet, where the guilty King tries to pray, and cannot. Haunted by fear, rather than remorse, he seeks privacy, retiring to his chamber, where he will not be interrupted. It is a solemn act, and a solemn moment, for he goes

to confess to himself, kneeling. /How easy it .
would be to depict a back ground in keeping—the
picturesque desertion—the shadowed—the solitary
light. Instead, what have we ? A great 'set scene'
is to follow ; so this oratory scene must be a carpenter's one—a cloth very far forward in front,
with an arch cut in it, to make room for a sort of
altar. The cloth waves—as the men pass behind,
. while the subdued sounds of hauling on great set
pieces, disturbes the King's orisons. As for the
scene itself, it is usually put close to the footlights,
but it is a passage, rather than a room, and those
front cloths are so close to the audience, that any
attempts at perspective look absurd. So they
certainly appear what they are, namely, a curtain
hung down till what is going behind is got ready.
And there the King prays, racking his conscience.
Under such conditions, is there, or can there be
any befitting *vraisemblance ?* Nay, the very
system of great ambitious 'sets' with the
necessary ' carpenter's scene ' each, so as to give
time for the ' setting '—is a lame and clumsy device when the awkward cloth descends, and
thrusts the characters on to the footlights. What
is this obvious screen intended for ? The very
sounds that come from behind the scene, when
some large set is being hauled into its place by a
corps of men, the strainings, creakings, rollings of
wheels, shouts of command, the swaying of the
curtain, all have their effect on the mind of the
spectator,and give to the result of these preparations

importance that overpowers the dramatic business.
When the curtain discloses some interior of a great
mansion, with steps, arches, recesses, windows,
regularly built, and all with a view of Sir John or
Lord A— having some conversation with his wife
or son, or various guests, we feel a sense of waste
—some tremendous Homeric action being expected.
The action too has the air of being contrived purposely. Often too, the drama suffers from this
tyranical exigence, and the action is distorted to
suit the demands of the scene painter. Thus it
is that Shakspeare's plays suffer particularly, as he
did not write in view of the arrangements to
which he is compelled by modern managers to
submit. Hence the modern difficulties of dealing
with his plays where there is ever a quick succession of short scenes, which must have supplied a
vivacity and movement which we moderns are
never indulged with. The first four scenes of
the ' Twelfth Night ' are singularly short, and the
changes are from the open air to the ' Duke's
House,' to the ' Lady's House,' and, to the Duke's
back again. Now the labour and noise which
attend a change of scenes, necessary in this way,
would destroy all illusion, and have a fretful dis-
tracting effect. The impression left would be, that
the trivial business was not worthy such ' a pother.'
But could not the action go on marked by changes,
noiselessly and quietly done ? It would be no more
than what the reader feels when he turns over the
page. The truth is this, ' scene turning,' and

changing business has encroached on the play when it ought to be subsidiary. The old system of 'cloths' and flats, rude as it was, answered this end far better. No matter how short the scene, or succession of scenes, there was the conventional screen behind, always ready. But so monstrous, Herculean, and costly has the system of changing scene become, requiring a hundred or two of stout arms on the stage, that the tendency is to confine every scene to its own act, and thus the brisk motions and shiftings of dramatic action are curtailed.

Another matter connected with this is that the 'building up' system throws everything out of proportion, and dwarfs the scene. If we look at buildings in a street in their reference to human figures, we shall see that they lie afar off at the back, while buildings close by us rise so high as to scarcely fall within the range of the eye. Yet our scene constructors contrive to bring every-thing—near and distant—within the same focus. The complete buildings close by, of which in life we could only see little beyond the base, are given in their completeness. On the cloths, however, distances, receding buildings, the idea of space, all may be supplied with perfect nature and success.*

---

* One is often astonished, even in the most elaborate ambitious 'sets,' to note the rudeness and dimension of the fitting together of the two systems—the old and the new. For we find the former usually retained for the upper part of the scene; the roof being portrayed by means of 'sky borders' or cloths, that hang down

The truth is, in real life, when, if we look at a street with buildings, there is a general indefiniteness—the details are merged in shadows and distance. Of the remarkable picture of Hypatia which was lately in the Grosvenor Gallery, it was remarked, that the figure is well drawn, and all the accessories, in no way slurred, have been carefully subordinated to it, so that it is on Hypatia herself the eye rests, not on the marble mosaics, and the hangings of the church. This is surely the true principle for the stage. We should be dimly conscious that marbles and mosaics were there, but they should not be intrusive or distinct. And here it is noticeable how the accurately panelled or moulded images of such things fail. In real life—the details being in relief—they have their minute shadows—which at a distance suggest this notion of detail which is yet indistinct. But in the case of the painted details the 'third dimension' is lacking: this indistinctness and blending is wholly wanting. The flood of light makes them obtrusive, and in the case of moulded detail they are all false in perspective, owing to their filling a space about a third the

in a series one behind the other, and painted in perspective, whereas below the built up scenes stand at various angles. There is no attempt at joining these discordant elements, or at illusion, and the whole has the effect of lengths of canvas, touching the tops of the screens. So, too, with those elaborate stately interiors of grand chambers in mansions and palaces, where there is, say, a monumental fireplace reaching to the ceiling of Renaissance pattern. This is often literally *laid* against the canvas-wall, with a space open between, owing to the warping of the wood. And so with many of these decorations which tell plainly that they have been 'carried on' by the carpenters and laid in their place.

size of what they would fill in real life. It is the very elaborate pretension of scenery that betrays its poverty. Again, as Lamb hints in a short but very pregnant passage, it is assumed from the effect which obtains in painting, that when the latter is transported to the stage the same result will follow. But he says truly, 'painting is a world in itself,' *i.e.* complete within the four corners of the frame. There is no attempt to deceive, and we are not invited to assume we are looking at a substitute, for say, real trees and houses. But on the stage, as Lamb says, 'there is the discordancy never to be got over *between painted scenes and real people*;' and he might have added that greater discordancy between the real boards or ground, that almost fixed area so many feet wide, and the vast painted distances: for, by retiring 'up,' hills are brought to the same height or level as a pillar, which should be three times the actor's height; or one may be standing beside a column whose shading only represents its circular form, which the actor's own solidity renders more feeble of effect.*

* This has been fully insisted on by Mr Parker, who, in his late work on the Nature of the Fine Arts, shows ingeniously how false to art is the mere imitation, so as to deceive, of ordinary objects, for that in painting this 'third dimension' of relief is not required. He shows that the somewhat artificial character of theatrical elocution corresponds to this absence of 'relief,' of the third dimension. Hence all things on the stage should be regulated by the one principle, so as to be in harmony, and the introduction of realistic matter makes the rest discordant and unnatural. As an illustration, how often do we find the elaborately painted canvas wall set off with *real* curtains, which by contrast make the wall seem painted, while the wall makes the curtains discordant !

Scenes as painted now are in far too gaudy a key;
and combined with the fiercely blazing light, which
beats upon the player from above and below, cause
a sense of unreality and distraction.   With such a
background, the figures cannot stand out conspic-
uously; nay, they seem substanceless.   Though
scenes are now so much 'built up,' it is not noticed
that they are without shadows or recesses—a great
inconsistency.   And here Lamb's remarks on stage
dress, are quite consistent with his other principles.
Speaking of the elaborate corronation robe worn
by Macbeth—'but so full and cumbersome, and set
out with ermine and pearls, as our king wears
when he goes to Parliament.'   He asks, 'In the
reading, what robe are we conscious of ?   Some
dim images of royalty—a crown and sceptre—may
float before our eyes: but *who shall describe the
fashion of it ?'*   Such should be the feeling in the
theatre.

LAMB touches all departments of the stage: acting, scenery, writing, in succession, and though there is no strict method in his treatment, we find his system perfectly homogenous. The same principle is at the bottom of all his speculations—viz., that a literal transcript of what we have with us in life, is no gain, and offers no genuine interest. It will be interesting to see with what *finesse* he works this out when dealing with acting, where perfect imitation of external types is sought, and where instead of the *essence* being grasped, details of dress, ' make up,' eccentricities of speech and manner are seized upon.*

* As in that now very common stage character, ' The Family Solicitor,' invariably presented in the one way, as a yellow faced husky being, with a sapient monosyllabic manner. Yet of such there are endless species—which the student of character, by his own instinct can vivify and lend variety to.

P

At first sight his theory seems a little fantastical, being to the effect that the actor should convey to the audience (like Bully Bottom to the ladies when personating the Lion) that he is not wholly in earnest and does not intend all he says. No doubt he had in his mind that general—almost poetical elevation, or exaggeration—which is necessary in a play, and is the excuse for the high sounding verse and diction, as for the whole opportunities and para-phernalia of acting. This, as an actor can inform us, is almost opposed to the principles that regulate daily life and movement. Thus with the act of walk-ing on the stage, which must in a manner be *acted* or emphasized; otherwise ordinary walking would seem like shambling. Hence a sort of purposed stride appears like common walking—just as paint laid on the cheeks, seems to produce the effect of the average tint in daily life. The reason would appear to be the *conspicuousness* of the actor's posi-tion—the glare of light under which he moves, and the limited area over which his movements are descried, where everything must appear to have a purpose.

Now, this ' optique ' of the scene is not limited to material things; it applies to all the passions and emotions. In this rather misunderstood passage Lamb gives perhaps the most valuable instruction the actor could desire; namely, that the system of literally copying from life destroys the airy tone of comedy: for truth, half the entertainment of our life consists in the fact that we do not reveal our characters to one another, and that there is generally a contrast between a man's character and his bearing. This is really the foundation of all agreeable social intercourse, of persiflage, irony, and pleasantry. Earnestness, or literalness, is in fact foreign to all society, and disturbs the relation. On the stage Elia maintains in several places that this idea is carried out by a sort of correspondence with the audience, or rather by letting them see that you are not wholly in earnest. This might be best explained by the illustration of the two ways of expressing the hypocritical Joseph Surface. The invariable mode is to present a crafty, smooth, canting, insinuating personage. As Lamb says the spectators expect — 'a downright revolting villain — no compromise.' He must inspire a cold and killing aversion, show two aspects of his character — the hidden hypocrisy and the outward bearing — letting the inner nature escape him by a hundred little arts and accidents—as it were *malgré* himself. This would be intended for the audience and for their enjoyment. 'All that neutral ground of character,' he goes on, ' a link which stood between vice and virtue ; or which, in fact, was indifferent to neither—is broken up and disfranchised.' How pregnant, how significant this is of the happy indeterminateness and general absence of detail—which should fit the grand breadth of the stage. In real life is not one of the chief motives of interest in society—that sort of mystery which waits in our neighbour's character, who never reveals himself in downright fashion, or speaks as he really thinks, or shows his anger, vexation, enjoyment in the candid way average dramatists enforce. Half the excitements and surprises of life are indeed owing to this opposition between the reality and the superficial acting of men and women. A great deal of the dramatic charm and interest, on or off the stage, is owing to this double operation. On the stage the dramatist or actor lets the audience into the secret of the character of the personage, or into that of the true meaning behind the particular utterance—though the actors are assumed to be ignorant of it. More interesting still is when we see a lack of correspondence between the character, its utterances and acts, owing, not to an intentional lack of truth and to a purpose to deceive, but to the influence of prejudices, the weaknesses of vanity, anger, &c. · Here we enter the field of comedy. To this department belong irony, sarcasm, persiflage, assumed indifference under attack, repartee, &c. In social life, no one who is injured openly threatens revenge, or reveals his private hatreds, or puts on the leering hypocrisy of a Maw-worm, or 'cants' after the stage fashion of Mr Surface. This is *surely* the meaning of Lamb's excellent exposition of the old mode of acting this famous comedy. Joseph was a hypocrite and a canting one, but did anyone in society cant according to the established histrionic traditions, he would cease to be a hypocrite. He would not be listened to, or allowed to impose on anyone. The player's argument seems to run—'My character is hypocritical, my only way of letting the audience know this is by presenting myself as such in speech and bearing'—a false theory. Now, in real life there would be speculation as to such a man; his friends asserting that he was genuine, his enemies that he was a humbug, He would have a candid plausible air, perhaps frank, and so far resemble honest men.

How different all this from the accepted stage mode, the upturning eyes, the sing song of the voice, duly labelled, or 'acted villainy.' This seems surely something of that intelligence with the audience which Lamb insists on, and that 'double intention' which lends such a charm to comedy. The relations of the spectator to the persons on the stage is that of a bystander, and that 'fourth wall' of the room is behind the audience, enclosing both him and the players. He is let into the secret of the real characters, and a great part of his entertainment consists in watching or speculating. 'Sir Peter' must be no longer a comic idea of a fretful old bachelor bridegroom—he must be a real person, capable, in law, of sustaining an injury; to realize him more, his sufferings under his unfortunate match must have the downright pungency of life, must make you uncomfortable, yet mirthful, just as the same predicament would move you in a neighbour or old friend.'

If then, the player is not to *reveal* himself or his character, how is the audience to know what his real

nature? This he enforces by his favourite theory,
of a *sub-intention*, or this half-intelligence with the
audience. Thus, Jack Palmer he describes as having
two voices, one for the audience, a peculiar tone by
which he marked certain things, as in italics. This
double or mixed class of character is a *caviare* to
many of our modern performers, who must play the
part one way or the other, an excellent instance of
which is furnished by Johnson's criticism on
Garrick's Archer, who portrayed a gentleman
disguised as a footman. Too often we find the player
identifying himself with the livery he wears, waiting,
handing, &c., with all a menial's art; sometimes indeed,
he raises a laugh by some act of comic awkwardness,
but his aim is on the whole, as described, the
mimicking of a servant. Yet, this single line of
Johnson's opens a new direction, 'the gentleman
does not break through the footman'—*i.e.*, he
should act the part, not as a footman, but as a
gentleman that is playing a footman — the *real*
character breaking through the assumed one, much
as the figure shows itself beneath the draperies.

The fine distinction drawn between the two
Palmers, the one's acting always suggesting 'a
gentleman, with a slight infusion of the footman;
the other with a still stronger infusion of the latter
ingredient,' though merely descriptive, is still a
distinction, for when the first was playing a servant, 'you thought what a pity he was not a gentleman;' and when the latter was playing an officer,
there had been a suggestion that he had been ad-

vanced from the ranks, all which points to that
double expression of character, which is such a
histrionic art—as when an actor is called on to
play such a character as a person originally of
low station—who had been promoted—or *vice
versa*, when a gentleman assumes the disguise of
a footman. Here, as Elia hints, the gentleman
should predominate, or, as we have said before,
break through 'the footman;' and, in the instance
of the promotion, the low element should struggle
with the superficial refinements. Yet how faulty,
tried by this test, have been the personating of
vulgar *parvenus*, by our most capable comedians—
it being conventionally established that the more
vulgar, and coarse, in speech, and action, the
more successful is the character. Yet, who in
his own experience of such persons in society,
has not noted that the vulgarity *escapes*, rather
than is spontaneously obtruded; for a person, who
has been clever enough to raise himself, will be
clever enough to make some attempt at imitating
good manners. He is betrayed too by a certain
awkwardness, and a palpable sense of discomfort,
and by attempts at being like the rest, which attempts fail.

The sketch of John Kemble playing Charles
Surface, supplies an admirable general idea of his
style of performance. He is here drawn to the
life. His 'weighty sense,' and 'exact declamatory
manners,' pointing the dialogue with precision, his
'sluggish mood and torpors,' husbanding of the

lungs ; which, however unsuitable, were to be pre-
ferred to the 'eternal, tormenting, unappeasable
vigilance' of modern tragedy. That is to the
fashion of making a point for every line, and
making business out of everything. At the same
time, he condemns 'that secret correspondence with
the company before the curtain, which is the bane
and death of tragedy, has an extremely happy effect
in some kinds of comedy, in the more highly
artificial comedy of Congreve, or of Sheridan,
especially when the absolute sense of reality (so
indispensable to scenes of interest) is not required,
or would rather interfere to diminish your pleasure.
The fact is, you do not believe in such characters
as Surface. If you did, they would shock, not
divert you.' Thus he does not mean here that
vulgar system of significant winkings and hint-
ings to the audience, but such an implied knowledge, conveyed by demeanour, as a bystander
at such a scene in real life would have.

The absence of responsibility in real life is
attractive enough, for the reason that there is a
pleasant piquancy in seeing our neighbours carry
off their responsibilities with due gaity or indifference—and this process, which gave the actor the
air of being out of *rapport* with his fellows, might
have seemed to Lamb to be a sort of *camaraderie*
with the audience. The illustration he supplies—
one of Ben the sailor, in Love for Love, asking
after his brother, quite forgetting that the news of
the latter's death had been written to him—surely

does not support his view. He considers that, in real life, such insensibility would shock us, and that, by the airy, pleasant tone assumed by the actor, his winking, as it were, to the audience, not to take him in strict earnest, the offensiveness is carried off. He further adds the reason that the character is a fancy one—unreal, compounded, and therefore outside the possibility of shocking us. But such 'outside nature' characters would not touch us at all, and would be regarded as curiosities in a museum. Rather Ben's character pleases us, because it is so natural, and the touch quoted is truly characteristic. It amuses, because we relish seeing the professional nature so dominant, that it overpowers, for the time, natural feeling. To this we could be indulgent in real life. The accepted element of wit, viz., surprise, enters here. We expect the conventional sympathy or grief, as we see it every day, and instead, find this careless-ness. It would certainly 'shock,' the audi-ence if it were a real instance of unfeeling nature, but as it is not, it is merely professional habit. That Lamb has some such view underneath his odd theory, is clear from what follows. 'But, when an actor displays, before our eyes, a down-right concretion of a Wapping sailor, when, instead of investing it with a delicious confusedness of the head, and ordinary indicated goodness of purpose, he gives to it a downright daylight understanding . . . then we feel the discord of the scene. The scene is disturbed.' He adds, curiously, 'A real man has got in among the dramatis personæ, and puts them out.' He surely means that the player interprets the character in too *literal* a way, making him as unfeeling as he can by laying emphasis on the forgetfulness of his lost relations.

A good instance of this realism of character, and which, seems out of place in real life, might be supplied from the comedy of the 'Twelfth Night.' At the close of the play, the befooled Malvolio, when quitting the gay scene of laughing courtiers, exclaims angrily, '*I will be revenged.*' This is often now delivered with a savage intensity that suggested the denunciation of Shylock. Yet it seemed out of key and keeping with the rest, and many might be puzzled to account for this impression. The steward was sensitive, quick to resentment, had been cruelly treated, and might naturally think of revenge. But, in real life, how would it be. Say in a country house, some guest has been made the butt of the company, and on an outrageous practical joke being discovered, pulls out a revolver : there would be a perfect panic in the house. But we readily conceive of some butt turning on his tormentors angrily, and saying, ' I'll pay you all out for this ! ' which would produce a roar of laughter, for all would know that this was but the vexation of the moment, and that genuine *revenge* was not thought of. There is, however, a danger in the excess of this principle. 'Comedians, paradoxical as it may seem,' says Lamb, 'may be too natural.' A most precious maxim, and well worth the actor's study.

Our gay well-tailored youths—lovers and brothers
—who come on in boating suits, or lawn tennis
'flannels,' will think this ludicrous or unintelligible;
but it truly destroys comedy. As our professor
lays it down, ' it is not that unbending thing.' His
illustration is the mirthful tale, where the teller
is allowed some latitude is in point, for how often
is the best of good stories spoiled by a certain
literalness in the telling, whereas a certain air of
irresponsibility and gaiety, commends it to the
listener irresistibly. Admirable, too, is the illustration of the annoyed man. A person resenting
being plagued and worried, excites our mirth.
We see contending feelings—a desperate wish to
appear unconcerned, the process of getting gradually angry *crescendo*. It thus remains whimsical,
whereas his expostulation ' in a tone that would
excite a duel,' only excites contempt or pity.

Lamb's sketch of Bensley in ' Malvolio,' is
familiar to every critic, and has a strange relish;
not because of its tribute to a respectable, though
rather obscure player, as from the value of the
rare critical distinctions it sets out. These have a
strange charm from their finesse and delicacy.
How admirable his enumeration of the *points* of
good acting, which, though felt, are so difficult
to describe in suitable words. Were any good
actor of our day to take this passage and study it
carefully till he sounded all its depths of meaning
what a profit—moral as well as pecuniary, he would
reap. For the principle pertains to the acting of

almost every character. He describes Bensley
seizing the moment of passion at the exact moment,
like a faithful clock never striking before the time;
his absence of stage artifice, coming on the stage to
do the poet's message, and his 'betraying none
of that cleverness which is the bane of serious
acting.' Every dramatic writer knows that there
is a special mode of putting forward speeches and
incidents on the stage ; things that read admirably
are found ineffective and even unintelligible, on
the stage. It is in truth another world, with a
language and beings of its own, with its own ways
and modes. It suggests indeed, that old-fashioned toy
where the objects are drawn distorted, to appear
quite correct and harmonious when looked at in the
proper way. This great art and mystery can
scarcely be taught. It is more an instinct, many
of the best 'acting' and most powerful situations in
the *repertoire* appear on reading to consist of a few
bald sentences with little point or colour, whereas
many an elaborate dialogue full of antithesis and
sparkle, have no result whatever, and sound flat.
The most curious contrast, however, is found between modern so-called dramatic dialogues and the
genuine work of Shakspeare and the great dramatists, where single utterances of the latter seem
to have no special point, and at the first glance to
be colourless, but in truth have the profoundest
significance, being appropriate to the character and
situation. An appropriateness that is further based
on large and general knowledge of human character,

and found on study to be what the character must utter in such a situation. It is thus in real life one might conceive of a most eccentric character, giving utterance occasionally to ordinary speeches. The modern system of play writing, on the contrary, is that the character must reveal itself in every utterance.

Again there is the great principle that it is the essence or quintessence of all things, which must be presented on the stage. The time is so short, and the attention of a large audience being a serious and important thing to demand, only what is strictly to the point, and representative may be offered, or if it do not fulfil these conditions, it will not command that attention. Mr Hayward used to lay down, that a good story should be '*cut to the bone, i. e.,* divested of all extraneous and unessential 'fat' or matter. As it is an epitome of life that is going on before our eyes, all that is trivial and unnecessary for the purpose in hand becomes impertinent. Above all, this principle of selection and abstraction being essential on the stage, only what is thus general, and because general at once recognisable, belongs to all ages and generations: the notes and tokens of human nature and character —these are what must be sought out and presented.

The description of Iago is full of delicate strokes; as — 'there was a triumphant tone about the character, natural to a general consciousness of power, with none of that petty vanity, which chuckles and cannot contain itself upon any little successful stroke of its knavery . . . . it was not a man setting his wits at a child, and winking all the while at the other children, but a consummate villain entrapping a noble nature . . . . where the manner was as fathomless as the purpose seemed dark and without motive.' What a light is here! What a revelation for an actor. He then passes to the well-known sketch of Malvolio, a delineation of delicate shades, is given, which, as a method, may be applied to other characters, and is a marvel of discrimination. Some of the touchings are exquisite in their delicacy. 'Malvolio is not essentially ludicrous. He becomes comic but by accident.' And again, ' he is cold, austere, repelling, but dignified, consistent, and his bearing is lofty, a little above his station. He is opposed to the proper levities of the piece.' These teachings would be an infallible guide to the intelligent actor, and in this spirit was it played by Irving. Unfortunately, the average actor is trained to a sort of code : as Lamb says elsewhere, he must be one thing or the other wholly—*entirely* comic or the reverse. There are no second or secret intentions with him. He cannot understand absurdities or comic utterance save as the expression of a comic soul within. Then as to the effect on the spectator thus produced; that 'smiling to himself' of Malvolio, as it is ordinarily personated, is meant to arouse the feeling, ' What an ass is this'—and induce the 'guffaws' of the gallery. And this is to be aided by a sort of ridiculous strut and grimacing, as though the player

was himself intent on exciting laughter. Yet thus,
Elia, 'What a dream it was! you were infected
with the illusion and did not wish that it should
be removed. You had no room for laughter,' which
opens an entirely different view. Again, take the
method of Dodd, one of the old actors. But first
let us think how one of our broadly humorous
'Comicks' works, when about to utter something
farcical; he is either solemnly grave, or with a
rollicking twinkle or leer 'pitches' his jest right
into the audience, or; in his own phrase, 'sticks it
into 'em.' Often he grins with them. He can gaze
stolidly too, when something is addressed to him he
does not comprehend, and then recognise the meaning with a sudden hearty burst. But turn to
Dodd. 'You could see the first dawn of an idea
stealing slowly over his countenance, climbing up
little by little, with a painful process, till it cleared
up at last to the fulness of a *twilight* conception.
He seemed to keep back his intellect, as some
have had the power to relax their pulsation. A
glimmer of understanding would appear in a corner
of his eye, and for lack of fuel go out again.' A
funny and intelligent performer like Mr Brough
would not fail to turn these marvellous writings to
profit.

Hamlet before giving his private theatricals, which
ended in such a scandal, it will be recollected, took
his performers aside, not merely to show them how
he wished his 'little piece' to be given, but for
some general instructions in the principles of their

profession. In depth and knowledge the admoni-
tions of the ill-fated Prince seem really to embody
the whole treasury of acting science. Nor are they
founded, as it might be thought, on technical
knowledge, or a long course of critical observation :
they are drawn from first principles common to all
views of human nature and human character, and
set out and enforced with marvellous sagacity. If
all our English actors were to diligently perpend,
comment, and thumb the single page on which
these directions are printed, they would find themselves in possession of all the knowledge that is
needful for their profession. Nay, even the dramatic author will find valuable principles under-
lying the few weighty hints Hamlet has thrown
out.

What an admirable and accurate description of a
well-constructed play does he give ! The first test :
' It was never acted ; or, if it was, not above once :
for the play, I remember, pleased not the million ;
'twas caviare to the general. How significant that
' for.' The manager, as it were, declined to take it,
as it went over the heads of the people   'Twould
not draw the crowd. Or one spirited manager
may have been induced to bring it out, but it did
not go beyond a first representation, and was then
withdrawn—a *succès d'estime*, in short. Many of
our great plays have experienced this fate—Goldsmith's, Sheridan's, and others. They have become
accepted, not by losing some of their *caviare*, but
by ' the general ' being educated into the ranks of

the particular, and learning by tradition and in-
heritance to relish the flavour. ' An excellent play,'
because written on true principles; 'well digested
in the scenes'—*i.e.* well constructed. Digested,
too, is a word of full and correct meaning, for the
process separates the essential; each scene therefore should hold so much as should carry forward
the piece. 'Set down with as much modesty as
cunning.' That is, as I conceive it, the writer
should not thrust himself forward in the conceits
that belong not to the character or plot, a test
which would put much modern writing 'out of
court.' And in this view it is worth noting the
development of the thought that follows: 'I remember one said there were no sallets in the lines
to make the matter savoury, nor no matter in the
phrase that might indite the author of affectation.'
The sense of which, leaving aside antiquarian
glosses, is clear enough. Our princely critic means
that there were no 'verbal *fireworks*,' as they are
called—repartees, *bon-mots*, etc., belonging to the
author, not to the character, to set off the situation.
The matter in hand was expounded with all sincerity and directness. Nor were the sentiments
garnished with flowers and far-fetched decorations;
nor, when the language was just and correct, was
there 'matter' or 'business' introduced which
would signify the author's humours or vanity.
The style or method should not tickle the ear with
conceits, but should be clear and classical; not
tawdry but simple; 'as wholesome as sweet—very

Q

much more handsome than fine.' Even this last
distinction between 'handsome' and 'fine' (that
is, between what is nobly dignified and merely
'showy')—as applied to writing—leads up to
much that is profitable.

It is when Hamlet comes to the players themselves
that his profound knowledge of the principles of
dramatic presentation become apparent. Let us
even take that phrase where he commends them
to the care of Polonius, calling them 'the abstract
and brief chronicles of the time,' hackneyed enough
as a quotation, and lightly quoted without any idea
of its meaning. That word 'abstract' is at the root
of all true acting. The vice of the ordinary players
is *concrete* or realistic acting, which is imitation. If a
policeman or a costermonger be brought on, the player
labours to present him *ad unguem* in his clothes,
mode of speech, and expression, giving a servile
copy of some particular specimen he has encountered.
So with those gentlemen and ladies who take tea
and play tennis. But the true personation of such
characters is founded on the general *type ;* and this
knowledge is only attained by study and comparison,
by which the *essential* characteristics are reached.
Otherwise the player will probably emphasize some
immaterial point found in the model, but not
peculiar to it. Hence, the result is flatness and
failure. All elements appear to be there—dress,
dialect, accent, extremes of speech ; but *character*
has been forgotten. A good instance can be found
in that masterly drawing of Macklin's, 'The Man of

the World,' whom the author had studied in the
different types of greedy scheming Scots who were
preying on the country in the days of Lord Bute,
and has shown the workings of the Caledonian
character under such conditions. Had Sir Pertinax
been drawn literally, exhibiting his grasping, greedy,
unprincipled nature, he would have been as revolting
as uninteresting, but these odious qualities are shown
disguised, as it were, and associated with so much
that is natural and humorous, that we almost
sympathise. An actor must be 'abstract' in this
sense; and the abstractness is only obtained by
constant observation. It must be noted also that
he styles them 'the *brief* chronicles' of the time.
That would signify, not that they presented a short
epitome by way of reflection of what was going on,
but the essentials—which was the essence, and had
significance and meaning. For much is now trans-
fered to the stage that is merely accident—not
significant in meaning: just as a logical mind will
in a few words give an exact definition of a
particular thing which it would take another a
whole page of description to portray, and which
would even then fail to convey any distinct idea.
This 'brief' and 'abstract' are not seen in imperfect
and inartistically constructed plays which find their
way to the boards. Again, events which fill an
ordinary act would never in real life be comprised
within so short a span. The writer should select
for his purpose events of a startling and amusing
kind, leaving out all neutral matter. But ordinary

life is merely dotted with exciting passages, and these take a long period for development. Here, indeed, is the true significance of a play. Passages of real dramatic interest but rarely fall within the experience of common life, which is, on the whole, prosy enough : and this excitement is what the stage professes to supply. This is what we pay our money to see. The dramatist, therefore, that merely transfers the average common incidents of life— real cabs, ladies and gentlemen at tea, and the like —may be realistic as he fancies he is, but is certainly unentertaining. No one really cares to see what he can see outside the theatre, though he may be a little surprised at the good imitation. As Johnson said of the dog walking on his hind legs, you do not admire the performance, but wonder at its being done. The art of the real dramatist consists in knitting together those events which ought to take long to develop, within a short compass, so artfully as to avoid huddling, and supplying the air of slow development. Another view of this 'brief' and 'abstract' lies in the strange pregnancy of colourless words and phrases, which stand, however, for action, intellectual or physical. The reader will pass them by, but behind them the action goes on, such as the often quoted '*Zaire tu pleures ?* '

The Prince's instructions in the art of acting which follow, are more in the direction of avoiding blemishes. But these, of course, become positive precepts. They concern (*a*) elocution, (*b*) rant, (*c*) gesture, (*d*) restraint, and (*e*) what is vulgarly called 'gagging;' within which circle of abuses are contained suggestions for making a good actor ; with, above all, (*f*) the purpose of acting and the stage itself.

(*a*) ELOCUTION.—'*Speak the speech, trippingly on the tongue.*' The meaning of this is shown by the caution against the abuse that follows. The delivery is to be animated and rather declamatory, but not to run into boisterous 'mouthing.' On the other hand, an equally great mistake is to suppose that the colloquial style of drawing-rooms and the streets are to be transported to the stage.

All the conditions of the stage are founded on exaggeration and a certain over-emphasis ; just as, to give the effect of natural everyday walk, it is necessary to assume a kind of laboured stalk. It is so with speaking. The conventional 'good-morning' and 'a fine day' tones are without effect. Even the strong glare cast upon the performers makes every movement and every glance of importance. And thus it is—the time being so short, and the attention being bestowed but for a very short time — trivial tones and trivial speeches sound *hors de propos*, and are out of keeping. 'Trippingly,' however—an admirable word — is what can barely be applied to the style of delivery of existing actors, which in many instances is slovenly and indistinct to a degree.

'*Mouth it*' unhappily needs no description, and is familiar enough in 'the provinces.' Still, if we come to preference, it is almost more 'to be endured' than the other vice; for it is an excess of a good thing. It is evident, indeed, from the whole spirit of the Prince's instructions, that this sort of 'rant' was the abuse of his time, as, indeed, it would seem to be of the stage generally in all times and places. Cumberland's well-known description of Quin's roaring and declaiming, shows that it applied just as fairly then; and even on the French stage at the present day the occasional extraordinary bursts of Mounet Sully approach the grotesque. Only on our own boards, singular to say, have we sunk into a sort of lethargic nonchalance. Some of this must be set down to the taste for familiar comedy as introduced by Mr Robertson; but the real cause lies deeper—to the want of instruction and lack of experience in our performers. Many of the younger London actors and actresses have had no training at all, and some could be named who, with no gifts but good looks, good address (and dress too), and good will, have obtained leading positions.

'*Use all gently.*' A golden rule indeed. '*Ne quid nimis.*' Reserve, or the 'Reserved forces,' in short, is the secret of power. The Prince lays this down in reference to gesture: '*Do not saw the air too much, but use all,*' etc. It is extraordinary, indeed, how, on the English stage, tradition seems to admit but two modes of expression—vehemence of voice, and vehemence of gesture; the extraordinary effects that can be produced by the face being

overlooked. Of course Mr Vaux-Clamant may
retort: 'What, no expression in the elevation of
my bushy eyebrows—in this haughty scowl—this
scornful curling of the lips? Go to!' These are
but elementary. Our protagonist has little notion
of what is alluded to. How few understand such
finesse as this: the sudden shiftings or contention
of emotion—*e.g.* an eager denial or self-vindication
—as the first impulse, to be checked by a doubt, as
the second? Or the distrust or uneasiness conveyed without frowning, or arching the brows, or
other gymnastics—allowing the sentiment to be
read in the face before the utterance? Again, the
expression by carriage, *air*, and manner.

' *In the torrent of your passion acquire a temperance.*' Here is opened a most interesting question
which has engaged the most thoughtful critics, viz.,
whether the player should trust to the impulse of
his passion, to 'its whirlwind,' or simulate it, thus
' begetting a temperance.' It was Johnson that
made the well-known speech, that if Garrick allowed
himself for a moment to feel like Richard III, he
deserved hanging on each occasion. But the truth
is such ' tempests,' by repetition, would soon lose
their spontaneous character, and the best opinions
declare that all should be duly and methodically
prepared. Of course, the actor should have the
general tone and feeling of his character, but the
path should be carefully marked out, and the
player ' keep on the walk.' All great orators have
prepared their speeches carefully: even their great

bursts have been, as it were, indicated beforehand ; the colouring, spirit, and vigour only being left to be supplied by the inspiration of the moment.

In this reserve, however, the opposite vice of 'tameness' is to be avoided, and a *juste milieu* secured. But how are our histrions to know ? Their ' own discretion is to be the guide.' But how, again, is this to be secured ? A really ' good thing' —that is, which secures a laugh—*vulgo*, '*fat*' in short—what average actor could sacrifice ? He must ' fetch ' the audience at all risks. If there be a thing notorious on our stage it is that the interests of the scene, that particular self-effacement for the good of the whole, is little thought of —as a custom, that is. Everyone fights for his own hand. Of course, I do not speak of the rare well-directed houses. But ' discretion' is indeed only the result of the highest and most careful training. It would take too long to discuss this point here, but it has been dealt with in a masterly way by Diderot, whom Mr Walter Pollock has translated. In an introduction to this volume, Mr Irving has set forth his views, based on his own large and thoughtful experience.

' *The robustious periwig-pated fellow*,' that tears a passion to rags, we have often seen in the provinces, where the groundlings delight in him. One or two popular peripatetics could be named who revel in this splitting of ears. Who does not sympathise with the Prince's bitter description of the ' groundlings '—the ' pit ' in those days—the

'gallery' as it used to be ? But at the present time,
when there is a general level of appreciation in all
parts of the 'house,' 'the groundlings' really
applies to that portion of the audience, which not
only enjoy 'noise,' but 'inexplicable dumb-show,'
perhaps those vacuous tenants of the stalls, the
patrons of 'leg-pieces' and a certain type of burlesque. This dumb-show, or 'shows,' for there are
both readings, is emphasized by the flourish of the
'toothpick and crutch,' and the relish of the
'awfully good' pastime presented — grimace,
tumblings, grotesque dress, the topical song, with a
burden pointed by slapping of hands, while a fellow
perforce does a 'breakdown'—surely these are 'all
inexplicable dumb-shows. and noise,' which our
refined groundlings are capable of, and the only
things they are capable of. Pit and gallery have
better taste.

'*Suit the action to the word, the word to the
action :*' an oft-quoted piece of advice, on which,
again, a separate essay might be written. To find
the proper action for the word, nay, to forbear
action wholly where action might be looked for ;
and how refreshing, how welcome, how infinitely
more significant than a page of speaking is a truly
significant action ! But this, again, is only found
by the nicest observation of human characters, and
perhaps a moment of inspiration. In the 'Princesse
Georges,' at the Gymnase, one of the performers
had to play a confidential butler, and after an
interview with his mistress, which leads him into

some strange speculations, he was told to withdraw.
As he reached the door, he stopped to raise the
wick of the *moderateur* in a fashion that seems to
convey his doubts and misgivings. There was an
apparent interest in the operation, but the state of
his mind was what was evident. There was also
the mechanical sense of duty as a pretext for lingering. But the simple action was so fraught with
meaning, and withal so delicately done, that a
burst of applause used to greet it nightly.

The purpose of playing ' *was to hold the mirror
up to nature.*' ' To *nature,*' mark, expounded, as it
were, by the succeeding words, 'virtue's scorn' (vice,
that is), and 'the age and body of the time.' Not
'dumb-shows,' it will be noticed, or 'noise;' he
means what is all intellectual, to the exclusion of
realism, or 'panorama.' It is curious indeed to see
how what is shown in the mirror of the stage
includes all that is really dramatic; for besides the
exhibition of what is good and bad, we have the
special features of the society of the time, whose
'form and pressure' is to be shown—that is, their
operation or action, which, from familiarity, would
escape the observation of ordinary persons, and
requires a writer of sagacity and knowledge to
extract and compress. Thus, in Sheridan's day, the
slaughter of reputations might seem to have become
so habitual as to be assumed to be a proper thing;
its 'pressure and form' was not seen in full odious
shape until he put his Sneerwells and Candours,
with Sir Peter's comments, on the boards. Passing

over what follows, as being a' repetition of stage exaggeration, we come to his last injunction—that concerning the leading 'comics,' your 'clowns.'

'*Speak no more than is set down for them.*' That they do not 'gag,' in short, or set on '*barren* spectators to laugh,' though some '*necessary question of the play be then to be considered.*' An admirable description both of the clowns and their audience — to be seen exemplified at many a theatre. Houses could be named where whole scenes are spun out by two of these mimics, 'capping' each other's gags, improvising antics and buffooneries. Meanwhile the play stands still. What was intended merely to be touched in a light way is magnified and lengthened beyond all proportion and the necessary question of the play which has been waiting becomes tedious by contrast, and is huddled over. That this, both in writer and actor, is the great vice is evident from Hamlet's words — the hardest he uses: '*That's villainous: and shows a most pitiful ambition in the fool that uses it.*' It applies to the writer as well, who in eagerness to 'set on *some* quantity of barren spectators to laugh' (and how pitiful to curry favour with only a small fraction of an audience), knows not how to practise restraint, but, got hold of a good thing, must needs put it all in at any length.

To take an illustration of this 'indiscretion,' there is that scene in Romeo and Juliet, where Mercutio utters the hackneyed burst about Queen

Mab. This is held to be a capital 'point' for the
actor, and he works it up accordingly, so as to
bring out, and illustrate every line—*e.g.*, wh·n he
comes to the word, 'drums in his ears,' it is *de
rigueur* to sound it 'd—r—r—ums.' At the close
there is applause, while the other characters who
have waited patiently, while this is being addressed to the audience, then resume their talk.
But a competent player, such as we speak of, reading
the scene in the true spirit, will see that the low-
spirited dreamy Romeo, is the centre of all. He and
his friends propose going to the masque; he
doubts, has presentiments, and dreams. At the
word, Mercutio rambles off into this pleasant description addressed to him in a light and airy,
but still serious strain, and carried away by his
theme—Romeo still indifferent, and in a reverie—
is going on, 'thus, this is she,' when the other
interrupts his friend—'peace, peace.' This form
is natural and poetical to a degree, it fits with the
sad character and tone of the scene, which is intended to forebode evil. How different from the
vulgar interpretation; it almost seems a boy's
spouting piece, delivered to the pit, by a boisterous
man. This is in truth in the spirit of what Lamb
has laid down on a corresponding occasion. Men-
tioning another favourite bit of declamation, where
the performer interrupts the business of the scene
to address the audience, viz., 'She never told her
love,' he says of Mrs Jordan, 'It was no set
speech that she had foreseen, so as to weave it

into a harmonious period,' but when she had
declared her sister's history to be a blank, and
that she never told her love,' here was a pause
as if the story had ended; then the image of the
worm i' the bud came up as a new suggestion and
heightened image — patience still followed after
that. Admirable precepts, indeed, and commending
themselves without argument. Or take the familiar
' All the world's a stage,' how detestable as a lugged-
in-speech — all the courtiers waiting, the sylvan
business interrupted, while the melancholy Jaques
'spouts' with suitable illustrations! These, and
many more such the judicious actor may develop
for himself out of these admirable councils.

The actor will note this admirable criticism :
'She was particularly excellent in her unbending
scenes in conversation with the clown.' (The
Lady in 'Twelfth Night.') 'I have seen some
Olivias,' he goes on, ' and those very sensible
actresses, too, who, in their interlocutions, have
seemed to set their wits at the jester, and to vie
conceits with him in downright emulation.' Who
has not seen this or something analogous in a
situation of the kind, each actor striving to make
his retorts *tell*, and excite approbation? The
superficial performer, in the part of Olivia,
would think she was doing admirably in ' putting
the clown down.' But as Lamb explains it, we
are lifted to a higher walk. His view is founded
on human nature. Due allowance, however, must
ever be made for the pressure of stage conventions,

which force the player to score every point that he
can. 'But,' goes on Lamb, 'she used him for
her sport, to trifle a leisure sentence or two with,
and then dismissed him.' The actress now-a-days
allotted the part has only to take this instruction,
and find a key to the whole character. Nor need
she suppose that it meant merely the reserve of
high rank; for there is beside an unbending good
humour. How, then, was familiarity to be avoided?
Let us read. 'She touched the *imperious fantastic humour* of the part with nicety.'

So in his account of Dodd, Lamb points to
a department, as it may be styled, too much
neglected by our performers; namely, facial and
corporeal expression. This is well-known and
cultivated with great art on the French stage,
where it, indeed, furnishes one chief enjoyment.
It is based, too, on the habits of daily life society.
Some embarrassing proposal is made of a sudden,
and we see plainly in the face, a confusion, a
struggle, a sense of annoyance, at variance with
the courteous tone in which the answer is made.
In 'Tricoche and Cacolet' there is a certain duke
who disguises himself as a servant, and his own
munificent instincts prompt him to discharge
various inconvenient debts of his mistress. As
these, however, multiply and increase in amount,
his feelings become mixed; as she tells him gravely
to pay the milliner—who is waiting—a very large
bill, his face assumes a rueful cast, then one
of annoyance, then of half-amused vexation, then of

contempt for himself, as who should say, 'I am
donkey myself to do this, but here goes,' and with
an assumed eagerness, his hand goes to his pocket,
and he pulls out his purse.   On the English stage
this amusing pantomime would be dispensed with,
there would be gestures of dissent and anger, and
the money would be given at last with a sort of
disgust and 'fuss.'   But the *finesse* I have described
is exactly in Lamb's manner in his account of
Dodd.   What a *subtlety* in the expression '*slowness
of apprehension.*'   This surely is a valuable instruction, if the actor would learn how to
develop the hint.   Describing his meeting with
Dodd in Gray's Inn Gardens, he again confesses to these powers of expression.   He has
the 'same vacant face of folly that looked out so
formally flat in Foppington, so frothily pert in
Tattle, so impotently busy in Backbite, so blankly
divested of all meaning, and resolutely expressive of
none in Acres, in Fribble, and a thousand agreeable
impertinences.'   It is astonishing, indeed, how
Lamb attained to such a knowledge.   In that comment on the playing of 'Twelfth Night' there is a
histrionic philosophy that might be expounded into
a science.   The actor who had mastered, and could
apply these precepts would be a first-rate performer
or at least a judicious one.

CONNECTED with these theories, but a little fantastic, is his well-known vindication of the loose dramas of Wycherley and Congreve, which the Restoration seemed to discharge, like sewage, over the fair theatrical pasture lands. This pleasant thesis he works out in his delightful fashion, much as his own 'Jack Palmer' might do, and, indeed, the whole description suggests Congreve himself, and has the smack and flavour of the comedy, which he so praises. He seems himself to speak with these 'two voices' he has been expatiating upon, and to be interpolating aside to his listeners that they are not to take him as being wholly in earnest. This, 'taking an airing beyond the diocese of the strict

conscience'; this 'not living always in the precincts of the law courts,' the imagining a world
with no 'meddling restrictions,' with characters
who break no laws and conscientious restraints,
'because they know of none,' and have got out of
Christendom into the Utopia of gallantry, where
pleasure is duty, and the manners perfect freedom,
and where no good persons can be shocked, for the
reason that 'no good person suffers on the stage,'
all such arguments cannot be accepted as serious.
'The great art of Congreve,' he says, 'is shown by
excluding any pretence to goodness or morality
whatsoever. Everything is in harmony, for there
is a general level of immorality undisturbed by a
single wholesome leaven. We accept and are
pleased with this strange state of things. Why?
Because "we are only a chaotic people," and who
are not to be brought to the standard of morals
that exists among the spectators. No revered
institutions are insulted by their proceedings, for
they have none amongst them; no peace of families
is violated, for no family ties exist among them.
. . . . Of what consequence is it to virtue, or
how is she at all concerned about it, whether Sir
Simon steals away Miss Martha, or who is the
father of Lord Froth's children.'

It is a sufficient answer to this pleasant fooling,
that our whole ground of interest in the stage is
founded on its being the response to our own
sympathies, and the reflection of our own feelings.
It is not then, 'a passing pageant, where we should

R

sit unconcerned,' but concern is essential to our entertainment. This interest should be found in what is common to all, but only an audience of rakes could relish the productions alluded to. But Lord Macaulay has, in fact, disposed of these airy pleas, which he justly dismisses as ' sophistical.' He shows clearly, what indeed our instinct assures us of, that comedy is a world in which morals play their part, and 'if comedy be an imitation, how is it possible that it can have no reference to the great rule which directs life, and to feelings which are called forth by every mode of life.' 'The heroes and heroines have a moral code of their own, an exceedingly bad one, but not as Mr Charles Lamb seems to think, a code existing only in the imagination of dramatists. It is, on the contrary, a code actually received and obeyed by great numbers of people. We need not go to Utopia or fairyland to find them, the morality of the Country Wife and the Old Bachelor is the morality, not of an unreal world, but of a world which is a great deal too real. And the question is simply this, whether a man of genius, who constantly and systematically endeavours to make this sort of character attractive . . . does not make an ill use of his powers.'

We find Lamb carrying this fantasy still further, taking the self-created delusion from the stage into real life. Speaking of Elliston's pleasant weakness of carrying on his acting off the stage— this pleasant conceit occurs to him, fit supplement for that Utopian standard of stage morality which he had created in vindication of Congreve and Wycherley. ' Did he play Ranger, and did Ranger fill the general bosom of the town with satisfaction, why should *he* not be Ranger, and diffuse the same cordial satisfaction among his private circle. Are we to like a pleasant rake or coxcomb on the stage, and give ourselves airs of aversion for the identical character presented to us in real life ?' As there was an artificial standard of morality on the stage, which was not to disturb us because it was different from that of the gospel, and because it entertains us, so, in real life, we might also accept false and artificial manners, because they were agreeable and dramatic. One would be inclined to doubt if these theories were mere pleasant fantastical exercises after all, if we consider some other opinions revealed to us by the essayist. There is a piteous, despairing genuineness in that burst of his, when he declares that he is in love with the earth and its pleasures, and could not bear the notion of leaving it, and that its joys bounded all his desires. This, in itself is a base, degrading shape of morality, and may supply a key to that tolerating plea for the corruptions of the dramatists.

LAMB'S delineation of Elliston's character, in itself a fine piece of comedy, is an illustration of his own theory. It dwells prominently on the memory, like Marlow or Sir Peter Teazle, or any of these familiar characters. Elliston, if literally painted, would appear in these colours as a loose debauchee, a bad husband and father, a spendthrift, a borrower, a drunkard, a vain egotist, and a sort of buffoon, whose absurdities, uttered gravely and without consciousness of the ridicule, caused perpetual amusement to his friends. Now, a character made up of such elements and offered on the stage would be as repulsive as uninteresting; it might be minutely elaborated by a professional hand, but the effect would be common-

place, much as that of 'a real hansom cab' driven
on to the stage. But when one with real artistic
insight comes, he does not bring 'him into court,'
as it were, or 'makes him capable' of suffering
serious injury at law; he seizes on the light airy
careless view with which society contents itself in
such matters, and thus Lamb, after his own theory,
seems to appeal 'aside' to the audience; 'we know
that he is a spendthrift, scapegrace, rake, &c., *au
fond*, but see the pleasant quaintness and humorous
contrasts of the character in the man!' And so
it would be in real life. There would be the two
views, one that of say the outraged wife, and
family, friends, and protectors who would see but
a shameful course of life, lacking in everything
that was really decent: the other that of the
acquaintance based on occasional contact, which
had only to do with these unconsciously developed humours and contrasts of character.
Here, too, would be illustrated his other theory
of the *innocence* of the Elizabethian dramatists, for
Elliston, like their heroes, seems to belong to that
artificial world where the moral sense is tem-
porarily suspended 'the Utopia of gallantry, where
pleasure is duty, and the manners perfect freedom.'

In this wonderful portrait Lamb shows that he
possesses a gift, such as he has described in Congreve,
Wycherley, and other dramatists, of abstracting
characters from life, and setting them before us
with art. To few is now the name of Elliston
known, and the fewer still who are familiar with

his character, hold him to be a sort of half-bur-
lesque, half - serious creature, not always sound
in his wits, and generally bemused with drink.
They accepted his astonishing bombast and jocose
solemnities as his humour.   But a few touchings
from Elia — a delicate analysis applied, and we
find the key to the whole in that interpretation,
which makes the character at once a delightful
original acquisition, such as we would not part
with, and certainly falling within the highest
comedy.   Such is the charm and power of the
skilled interpreter, who thus skilfully expounds
character.   There are a number of humorous
stories retailed of this actor, his solemn replies,
full of a grotesque pretence, which sound to many
positively of a half-cracked nature.   But to this
pleasant analyst the true reading came easily.
He saw at once the *double* side to this nature ; the
genuineness of his pretences.   Elliston, according
to his reading, is exactly what is one of the gay
creatures in Congreve's or Wycherley's scenes.   In
real life, he applied that pleasant levity, that 'only
half in earnest,' which makes the charm of comedy
acting.   His defence, then, is in itself, delightful
comedy.   'Are we to like a pleasant rake or coxcomb on the stage, and give ourselves airs of
aversion for the identical character presented to
us in real life?   But we want the real man.   Are
you quite sure that it is not the man himself whom
you cannot see under some advantageous trappings?'
It truly belongs to the stage to conceive of that

harmonious fusion of the manners of the player into those of everyday life, which brought the stage boards into streets and dining parlours. It may be conceived how this pleasant delusion would operate on a peculiar character. This was different from Garrick, of whom it' was said that it was only off the stage he was acting, but on the stage was natural, easy, and affecting. Elliston was acting both on as well as off the stage. But there is a nice discrimination, or distinction which might have escaped Goldsmith, for the ' acting,' as applied to Garrick, is used in a more professional sense—as a token of insincerity. But Lamb's idea of Elliston off the stage was that gay levity which offered assurances with an earnestness, and at the same time, a smiling glance at the pit, as who should say ' Don't trust me.'

The traits and stories, which made such an impression on Lamb, are amusing from the very fashion of the telling. His 'great style ;' 'Have you heard the news,' the story of the dinner, ' reckoning fish as nothing;' these things, and many like them, have been retailed in the memoirs, as pieces of absurdity or brag, and which made his friends laugh. Yet, who but Lamb could have given such an explanation of this last jest, of what was within —' the manner was all. It was as if, by one peremptory sentence, he had decreed the annihilation of all the savoury esculents,' &c. There is a story of his that would have delighted Elia, had he heard it, it was also in his ' great manner.' The manager

was about to retire, when the King, condescendingly,
added his wishes for the lessee's success in his
theatrical government; on which Elliston, by one
of those strange impulses so peculiar to him, re-
plied, 'If *you*, sir, are *loyal*, I must obtain a
triumph.' This was the regal style. Here the
pleasant reversal of the relation—the sovereign
.being invited to be 'loyal' to the subject, would
have assisted Lamb largely. In this essay there
are further glimpses of the true essentials of
comedy, and of the appreciation of the art of the
great masters of comedy. As in the sketch of
the actor, as librarian at Leamington — strictly
founded on fact. ' So have I seen him,' he, after an
exquisite sketch of Elliston, 'expatiating on his
goods to two lady visitors—a gentleman in comedy
acting the shopman. I admired the histrionic art
by which he managed to carry clean away every
notion of disgrace from the occupation he had so
generously submitted to.' Here we have Johnson's
canon, as applied to Garrick, in Archer, of letting
the gentleman break through the footman, and
it may be repeated, that the player, who studied
this sketch of Elliston, would find himself enriched
with new interests, which could be applied—say,
to such a character, as 'Young Marlow,' with its
double course of whims and humours; the shy
nature exhibited to the company, the bold and im-
pudent to the supposed barmaid, and at other times
the one ' breaking through the other.'

[Lamb indulges in the following rhapsody on his favourite, which, as it contains nothing didactic, has been omitted from the collection of dramatic essays.]

JOYOUSEST of once embodied spirits, whither at length hast thou flown ? To what genial region are we permitted to conjecture that thou hast flitted ?

Art thou sowing thy WILD OATS yet (the harvest time was still to come with thee) upon casual sands of Avernus ? or art thou enacting ROVER (as we would gladlier think) by wandering Elysian streams ?

This mortal frame, whilst thou did play thy brief

antics amongst us, was in truth anything but a
prison to thee, as the vain Platonist dreams of this
body to be no better than a county jail, forsooth, or
some house of durance vile, whereof the five senses
are the fetters.   Thou knewest better than to be in
a hurry to cast off those gyves; and had notice to
quit, I fear, before thou wert ready to abandon this
fleshy tenement.   It was thy Pleasure House, thy
Palace of Dainty Devices; thy Louvre, or thy White
Hall.

What new mysterious lodgings dost thou tenant
now? or when may we expect thy aërial house-
warming?

Tartarus we know, and we have read of the
Blessed Shades; now cannot I intelligibly fancy
thee in either.

Is it too much to hazard a conjecture that (as
the Schoolmen admitted a receptacle apart for
Patriarchs and un-chrishom babes) there may exist
—not far perchance from that store-house of all
vanities, which Milton saw in a vision—a LIMBO
somewhere for PLAYERS? and that

> Up thither like aërial vapours fly
> Both all Stage things, and all that in Stage things
> Built their fond hopes of glory, or lasting fame?
> All the unaccomplish'd works of Authors' hands,
> Abortive, monstrous, or unkindly mix'd,
> Damn'd upon earth, fleet thither—
> Play, Opera, Farce, with all their trumpery.—

There, by the neighbouring moon, (by some not
improperly supposed thy Regent Planet upon earth,)
mayst thou not still be acting thy managerial

pranks, great disembodied lessee ? but lessee still, and still a manager.

In green-rooms, impervious to mortal eye, the muse beholds thee wielding posthumous empire.

Thin ghosts of figurantes (never plump on earth) circle thee in endlessly, and still their song is *Fie on sinful phantasy!*

Magnificent were thy capriccios on this globe of earth, ROBERT WILLIAM ELLISTON! for as yet we know not thy new name in heaven.

It irks me to think, that, stript of thy regalities, thou shouldst ferry over, a poor forked shade in crazy Stygian wherry. Methinks I hear the old boatman, paddling by the weedy wharf, with rancid voice, bawling 'Sculls, Sculls!' to which, with waving hand and majestic action, thou deignest no reply, other than in two curt monosyllables, 'No: Oars.'

But the laws of Pluto's kingdom know small difference between king and cobbler, manager and call-boy; and if haply your dates of life were conterminate, you are quietly taking your passage, check by check (O, ignoble levelling of Death !) with the shade of some recently departed candle-snuffer.

But mercy ! what strippings, what tearing off of histrionic robes and private vanities ! what denudations to the bone, before the surly Ferryman will admit you to set a foot within his battered lighter !

Crowns, sceptres, shield, sword, and truncheon,

thy own coronation robes (for thou hast brought
the whole property-man's wardrobe with thee,
enough to sink a navy), the judge's ermine, the
coxcomb's wig, the snuffbox *à la Foppington*—all
must overboard, he positively swears; and that
Ancient Mariner brooks no denial; for, since the
tiresome monodrame of the old Thracian Harper,
Charon, it is to be believed, hath shown small taste
for theatricals.

Ay, now 'tis done. You are just boat-weight;
pura et puta anima.

But, bless me, how *little* you look!

So shall we all look—kings and keysars—stripped
for the last voyage.

But the murky rogue pushes off. Adieu, pleasant,
and thrice pleasant shade! with my parting thanks
for many a heavy hour of life lightened by thy
harmless extravaganzas, public or domestic.

Rhadamanthus, who tries the lighter causes
below, leaving to his two brethren the heavy calen-
dars—honest Rhadamanth, always partial to players,
weighing their parti-coloured existence here upon
earth—making account of the few foibles that may
have shaded thy *real life*, as we call it (though,
substantially, scarcely less a vapour than thy idlest
vagaries upon the boards of Drury), as but of so
many echoes, natural re-percussions, and results to
be expected from the assumed extravagances of thy
secondary or *mock life*, nightly upon a stage—after
a lenient castigation, with rods lighter than of those
Medusean ringlets, but just enough to 'whip the

offending Adam out of thee,' shall courteously dismiss thee at the right hand gate—the O. P. side of
Hades—that conducts to masques and merry-
makings in the Theatre Royal of Proserpine.

PLAUDITO ET VALETO

WE are so accustomed to think of Lamb as an
essayist, that we are apt to overlook his very
intimate connection with the stage, and knowledge
of the drama. He was intimately acquainted with
the leading players. He wrote several plays, which
were produced or published, he criticised new pieces,
was perpetually attending the theatre, and has left
a body of official criticisms on the old dramatists,
together with the well-known essays on the stage
and the principles of dramatic effect. This taste
and great familiarity must have been of important
help to him; though it must be admitted, this
admirable knowledge of principles did not aid him
in practice, for there can be no doubt that his two
humorous farces are failures, 'flat' and pointless

to a degree. It is surprising to think how such a piece as 'Mr H.—' could have been accepted or produced—and a greater problem still is, how such a humourist could himself have accepted such specimens of dialogue—intended for humorous— as he puts into the 'Pawnbroker's Daughter.'

Even in the most trifling of Lamb's critical sketches, there is a delicate analysis, which suggests far more than it describes, and brings before the mind something in the shape of dramatic action. As in the case of Munden's delineation of the 'Cobbler of Preston,' where 'his alternations from the cobbler to the magnifico, and from the magnifico to the cobbler, keeps the brain of the spectator in as wild a ferment, as if some Arabian Night were being acted before him.' In interpreting such a situation, there would be with us the official system. As the magnifico, the cobbler, would be as droll and broadly comic as possible, taking the accepted 'business' of 'Bottom, the Weaver,' as his guide. But Lamb hints at opening up another region altogether; and what a wonderfully suggestive note for acting is struck in the following— 'Who, like him, can throw a penetrating interest over the commonest daily life objects. A table or a joint stool, in his conception, rises into a dignity equivalent to Cassiopeia's chair. It is invested with constellating importance. . . . So the gusto of Munden antiquates and ennobles what it touches. . . . A tub of butter, contemplated by him, amounts to a platonic idea. He understands a leg of

mutton in its quiditty.' In all which, is involved
a mystery of acting, little thought of or scarcely
believed in—viz: that of making the audience
believe, by the player's showing that he believes.
This really favours the performer himself—though
he appears to be working for another. To show that
he is affected by the delusion, is the best way to
affect others, and this being overwhelmed by
wonder, admiration, or belief in something, is a
powerful source of effect. This faculty in the case
of Munden was illustrated by a simple piece of
acting not set down for him, but which was a true
inspiration—a *play* itself! A pewter is on the
table, with which the player is alone. He says,
'some gentleman has left his beer,' and after a
little hesitation, drinks. But the fashion in which
this meagre text was worked out, was a marvel,
exhibiting the whole gamut of passions—first surprise and pleased recognition; then doubt, fear of
detection, resolve, hesitation again, greed, humour,
&c. If we here supply Lamb's description of
Dodd, the way in which the glimmer of an idea
would begin to dawn, and then spread over his
whole face, we shall see what power of true
acting can underlie even facial expression, and
how its incidents can almost be followed dramat-
ically. For many minutes, the progress of this
struggle was continued, the actor being drawn
gradually within the charm of the pewter and
its fascinations, until at last he succumbs. Yes,
in that simple sentence, there was an art—'some

gentleman has left his beer,' a simple statement of a historical kind, colourless, as it were; but the tone and expression of face, seemed an argument, or at least an expression of contending emotions. He has left his beer—not intending to drink it; or has forgotten it. Then why should not I—but then the risk, should he return. If I do not, some one else will—or, let me not heed the risk, and dare all!

That 'strangely neglected thing,' the Cobbler of Preston, even in this sketchy allusion, seems to bring before us at once something dramatic. We feel a sensation as if witnessing the play itself. The various turns and shifts would perforce operate on the actor of our day, whatever his talents, and bring out his resources. Thus, Kit the Cobbler having been found drunk by some gentlemen, they carry him to a fire, and play this trick on him.

(*The doors opened, the Cobbler discovered in a rich bed; servants on each side the stage.*)

Kit. (*yawning*).—Heigh-ho! a pot of small eale, Joan, for heaven's sake, a pot of small eale; why do'st not come, woman? Hey-day! what!—why certainly I am awake—Ah! what! I am most damnably frightened. I don't like these fellows; who are they? I dare not ask; no, not for the soul of me.

Enter Lorenzo.

Loren.—Is my Lord awake, Diego?
Diego.—Softly, Lorenzo, softly; he is asleep still.
Loren.—His Majesty has sent to know how he rested last night.
Kit.—I am most horribly frighted. The King sends to know how I rest! I am most damnably frighted.

(*Diego goes to the bed, and Kit sneaks his head under the bedclothes.*)

Diego.—Ten to one, now, when he awakes, he will ramble and rave as he used to do, about the story of the cobbler and his wife.

S

Kit.—A cobbler and his wife ! why, they can't mean me, sure, al this while !

Kit.—What the devil are they about ? Here is some cursed blunder made ; I shall be hang'd, that is certain ; I am got into a lord's bed-chamber, I don't know how ; ay, and into his very bed, I don't know when.—(*A strain of music.*)

Diego.—I will venture to peep once more, and see if he stirs yet.

Kit.—Ah, Lord, now I am taken in the fact.

Diego (*softly at his curtains*).—My Lord, my honour'd Lord.

Kit.—What does your good worship say ? Here is nobody here but I.

Loren.—Your lordship's gown.

(*They put on his gown and set him at the foot of the bed.*)

Diego.—Will your lordship taste some chocolate, or tea ?

Kit.—If you please, you mistake me for some other person.

Loren.—Ah ! Diego, Diego ! he is still in the same unhappy distraction.

Diego.—What clothes will your lordship please to wear to-day ?

Kit.—Pho ! what do you mean ? I am Christopher Sly, of Preston heath.—Nay, nay, do not gear a body thus.

Diego.—Your English brocade is too hot, and the Persian too cool ; I think your Genoa ash-coloured velvet will suit your honour best to-day.

Kit.—Spain ?—Am I a Lord ? And have I such a lady ? Or do I dream ? Or have I dreamed till now ? I do not sleep ; I see, I hear, I speak. Oh ! pooh ; it would be very rude and impertinent in me to doubt any longer. Well, bring our lady hither to our sight. And, prithee, friend, once more, a pot of the smallest eale.

Mar. How fares my noble lord ?

Kit. Marry, I fare well ;—here's cheer enough. But pray where's my wife ?

Mar.—Here, my good Lord. I have brought you a learned doctor. What is your lordship's pleasure ?

Kit.—Hah ! a goodly wench ! a *bana roba* in troth. Now shall I know whether this be a dream or no, in a moment. Are you my wife, forsooth ? Ah ! why don't you call me husband ? My men say I am a lord, and I am your good man.

Mar. My husband and my lord, my lord and husband. I am your dearest wife in all obedience.

Kit.—Very well : I am glad to hear it. What must I call her ?

Diego.—Madam, and nothing else ; so lords call their ladies.

Kit.—Madam, they say that I have slept and dreamt some fifteen years, or thereabouts.

Mar.—Yes ; and it seemed a tedious age to me.

Kit.—Hah ! that's much ! Servants leave me and Madam alone, before I take t'other nap. Madam wife, come and kiss me.

A Cobbler's Stall on one side of the stage, and a little poor bed on the other, Kit in bed ; a stool with the morning-gown ; a cobbler's working stool and tools. Boots, shoes, and galoshoes, &c.

Kit. (*alone*)—Hey oh ! where are my servants ? Here, some of you bring me a whole butt of your English small-beer. Here Diego! Lorenzo! Bartolino! why, where are my varlets? I'll have the dogs' liveries stripped over their ears, and turn'em all out to grass. Ah! what! why this is my old flock hammock! Ah, and there is my spacious shop too, of a yard long! now am I most consumedly puzzled, to know whether I dreamt before, or whether I dream now, or whether 'tis all a dream from beginning to ending? whether I am my lord What d'y' call him, or Kit the Cobbler? somebody or nobody?

Enter Joan.

Hold! here comes one who will interpret all my dream, with a vengeance.

Joan (busy sweeping and setting the room to right) Was there ever such a sot! All our neighbours cry shame o'en—wou'd he were here! I would rattle him! Good luck! What a litter this shop is in! We have a mort of work and not one stitch set; there's neighbour Clumps' boots to be liquor'd; there's Peter Hobson's shoe'n to be tapp'd; besides Dame Goslin's pattens, and the curate's galoshoes that are to be lin'd with swan skin. O Lud! Oh, thieves! murther! fire!

Kit.—How now! what, is the woman mad!

Joan.—Thieves, thieves!

Kit.—Silence, I say. What has possessed the woman? Either take that abominable shrill pipe of thine a note lower; or I will——

Joan.—Who are you? what are you? how came you here? and what business have you in this place?

Kit.—Ah!

Joan.—Oh! lud! Kit! why, I left thee just now fast asleep at the constable's house. I staid but one moment at Goody Tattle's, to tell her to take her cow out of the lees. And see if thou hast not slipt home, and got into bed before me!

Kit.—Let us hear that again!—Ah! where didst thou leave thy husband, good woman, dost thou say?

Joan.—Why, I tell thee, Kit, I left thee at the constable's, drunk asleep; and I marl how thou gottest home so soon!

Kit.—Haud ye! haud ye! Not so fast, woman. I will take care thy husband shall come to no harm: he is an honest man: he loves a cup of ale, I have heard; but that's a small fault. Go home, be easy; my servants shall bring thee thy husband.

Joan.—Thy servants! Out, ye drunken sot. Why, Kit, what do you deny your lawful wife, Kit? (*Crying.*) Oh, oh! was ever poor woman so used by a saucy knave.

Recalling the description of Munden we almost see how this droll part should be done. Not certainly after the pattern that most of our modern comedians would apply. The condition would be to make fun, to show a comic bewilderment, that would extract laughter. Thus, a modern 'comic,' getting into his royal robe, would make many sides ache. But this would not be *a la Munden*, or that complex web and warp of emotions—stupid bewilderment, delight, and enjoyment. And then, as Lamb points out— the extra bewilderment from the reversion to the old Cobbler's stall, and the renewed withdrawal from this again, which would end in fearsome bemuddlement !